Coming of Age in 2020

Teenagers on the Year That Changed Everything

COMING OF AGE IN 2020

Teenagers on the Year That Changed Everything

Edited by Katherine Schulten
of The New York Times

W. W. NORTON & COMPANY

Independent Publishers Since 1923

For information about permission to reproduce selections from this book,
write to Permissions, W. W. Norton & Company, Inc.,
500 Fifth Avenue, New York, NY 10110

For information about special discounts for bulk purchases, please contact
W. W. Norton Special Sales at specialsales@wwnorton.com or 800-233-4830

Manufacturing by Versa Press
Book design by FaceOut Studio
Production managers: Katelyn MacKenzie, Julia Druskin, and Gwen Cullen

ISBN: 978-1-324-01944-2 (pbk.)

Library of Congress Cataloging-in-Publication Data

Names: Schulten, Katherine, editor.
Title: Coming of age in 2020 : teenagers on the year that changed everything /
    from the New York Times Learning Network ; edited by Katherine Schulten.
Description: First edition. | New York : W.W. Norton & Company, [2022] |
    Includes index.
Identifiers: LCCN 2021061680 | ISBN 9781324019442 (paperback) | ISBN
    9781324019459 (epub)
Subjects: LCSH: Teenagers—United States--Attitudes. | Teenagers—United
    States—Social conditions. | Coming of age—United States. | COVID-19
    Pandemic, 2020—United States—Influence. | Two thousand twenty, A.D. |
    United States—Politics and government—2017-2021. | United States—Social
    conditions—2020-
Classification: LCC HQ796 .C687 2022 | DDC 305.2350973—dc23/eng/20220611
LC record available at https://lccn.loc.gov/2021061680

W. W. Norton & Company, Inc., 500 Fifth Avenue, New York, NY 10110
www.wwnorton.com

W. W. Norton & Company Ltd. 15 Carlisle Street, London W1D 3BS

CONTENTS

INTRODUCTION

EVERYONE KNOWS what coming of age in America is supposed to look like. Countless movies, books, and songs have told us.

Then came 2020. Instead of proms and championship games and all-night hangouts with friends, there was school on Zoom from bed. Outside a pandemic raged, an economic collapse threatened, political divides widened, and a racial reckoning sparked what is likely the largest protest movement in American history.

In this book, teenagers from across the country show you how they coped with a world on fire. Via diary entries and comics, photos, poems, and paintings, charts, lists, Lego sculptures, songs, recipes, and rants, they tell the story of the year that will define their generation.

As 16-year-old Samantha Liu puts it, "Making history is way overrated."

These 161 pieces were chosen from over 5,500 submissions sent in to a contest on The New York Times Learning Network, a site about teaching and learning with current events. In the spring of 2020, historians and museums were encouraging us all to record our pandemic experiences and keep artifacts for posterity. We editors wondered, what artifacts might teenagers be creating? What if we could provide a place for them to share their stories?

That fall we asked our teen audience, "What has 2020 been like for you?" We encouraged them to respond in whatever format they wanted—via words or images, audio or video. We challenged them to document what they were living through, and to express themselves creatively on any aspect that seemed important. Knowing that many would not think their experiences were novel enough to record, we also reminded them repeatedly that "there are stories only you can tell."

The result is this book, in which every contribution, whether heartbreaking, hopeful, fierce, or funny, offers a glimpse into a different life. A girl in Alaska doodles "raw emotions" in her diary. A boy in upstate New York photographs quarantine life on his family farm. Two friends in California have an awkward conversation in a Zoom breakout room. A boy in Minneapolis reflects on community after the murder of George Floyd. A girl in Brooklyn describes her terror as she and her family get sick.

In March of 2021, *The New York Times* published a special print and digital section of the newspaper featuring the work of 37 teenage winners of our contest. Now, in this expanded collection, we've included many more voices, to tell an even richer story. As we did then, we have organized the work chronologically and thematically, beginning with those eerie days of early March and running through the summer protests and November election.

Though each individual submission is a dispatch from a specific time, place, and point of view, this collection makes vivid what Generation Z suffered together. Again and again these pieces show us their loneliness, frustration, and despair; their fraying relationships; the numbing days of online school; and their deep anxieties about the future.

But equally vivid across every section of this book is their need to find meaning. The vast majority of teenagers who responded to our invitation found a way to reach for hope. They surprised themselves by bonding with family members, discovering nature, inventing new hobbies, and making art. They woke up to injustice, and came together in their power to fight it. In spite of everything, they told us, there was joy. In an upended year, they discovered things about themselves they might otherwise never have known.

For each submission, we asked for a short "Artist's Statement" describing when, where, why, and how the piece was created, and excerpts from those statements accompany all of the visual pieces. Reading them together, you can hear a generation's voice—raw, honest, and self-aware, playful, wry, and inventive. As Lauren Sanchez, 15, says, "We don't have past examples for how to come of age in a world like this, so we are figuring it out on our own."

Throughout the 2020–2021 school year, we heard from teachers across the country who used our related curriculum to host their own classroom versions of this contest. Many told us it was the most successful project they did,

a way of building community around a common experience while also allowing each student to say exactly what they wanted to say.

This book is a time capsule, a detailed record of how ordinary teenagers experienced extraordinary events. We can't yet know all the ways 2020 will shape this generation, but experts on trauma tell us we will all be processing what happened for decades to come.

Long after this crisis is over, in some happier future where teenagers are focused again on crushes and colleges instead of masks and vaccines, we hope this collection will still offer them inspiration—for documenting the big and small moments in life, for reflecting on who they are, and for getting their unique voices out into the world.

—KATHERINE SCHULTEN, editor,

The New York Times Learning Network

COMING OF AGE IN 2020

We are becoming adults in this year that is like no other.

    We don't have past examples for how to come of age in a world like this, so we are figuring it out on our own.

    We are living through struggles that the world has never seen and we are figuring out solutions the world has never thought of.

ADJUSTING TO A NEW NORMAL

"It began as a low buzz."

Excerpt from "The We in Worldwide" by Aryana Singh, 15, New York City

We were all lost at some point, with days sometimes feeling like weeks and weeks sometimes feeling like hours. No matter what, this pandemic has given us time to reflect upon ourselves.

"Crescendo" by Macy Young, 15, York, Maine

It began as a low buzz. A quiet yet constant hum. A slight nuisance. The ominous opening notes of a symphony, a hundred bows poised and the conductor's hands lifted in anticipation.

Corona. It was only a whisper. A name whose meaning was still widely recognized as an alcoholic beverage. A word that embodied vacation and relaxing summer days topped with a slice of lime. It was merely a hushed tone, the cry of a single violinist's bow across tight strings.

Slowly but surely the music swelled, the buzz grew louder, the screeching cry was joined by an army of instruments. Soon, the noise was deafening, the world was spinning, and that one word circled overhead like a descending helicopter, the whirring of its sharp metallic wings drowning out all else.

National Emergency. Apocalypse. Pandemic. Contagion. Outbreak. Plague.

Millions of words thrust into the air, lighting the fuse of a ticking bomb. Millions of voices growing louder and louder. Fear growing larger and larger. Uncertainty the most deafening presence of all.

Wedges of lime were no longer on the minds of masses. Each became isolated in their own worries and fears and doubt, yet the world was united in this universal uncertainty. None knew the answers yet all were together in this answerless-ness.

Deaths, cases, mortality rates, symptoms, charts, testing policies.

The answers once longed for, are now delivered like a punch to the gut. And even with these numbers, statistics, and protocols, uncertainty only grows, panic only rises, and the thunderous noise swells louder still.

Legs twitch and hands itch. Eyes dart and ears are filled with the *thump, thump, thump* of a racing heart. Spurred to action, convinced that there is something to do, a place to be, things to buy, and words to believe. Convinced that there is a use for legs burning to run and fingers itching to *do*. To *do* something, anything.

Yet despite this itching, burning, tingling, crawling urge to act, to run, to hide, to speak, to scream, to *do*, you find yourself sitting still. Looking out the window at the world spiraling into chaos just beyond the cool glass. You are unable to move.

Instead, you sit and you stare and you worry and you are quiet. You are quiet in a world of raging, roaring, deafening noise. Words and voices and screams dance in devilish pairs above your head. The sickly music booms louder and louder, but your mind is alarmingly quiet. Empty. Whitewashed with uncertainty.

It began as a low buzz. And now, now there is nothing louder than its constant roar.

These are messages of a conversation I had with my sister on March 24, 2020. It was the first time I went with my parents to our grocery store, and I forgot to wear the mask before wearing the hijab, so I texted my sister to ask her how and she explained it. Remembering to wear the mask first is something that I still struggle with to this day.

"The God of Toilet Paper" by Hayool Park, 15, Redmond, Washington

The toilet paper shortage was only a part of the struggle. At the beginning there was also no hand sanitizer, masks, or other supplies.

After going to several stores, I saw countless barren shelves in multiple kinds of sections. People were preparing for the worst. My artwork represents the craze.

Dear March 13th Lauren,

Today is the last day of being in public unmasked, the last day Dad drives you to school, the last day of seeing your friends without extensive precautions. Today marks the end of life as you know it. Savor today.

Until today, life has been average. You woke up, went to school, to rehearsal, did homework, and came home. Repeated the next day, and on and on. You planned to go to college, get a job, get married: the perfect cookie-cutter life. Your life was ordinary. Unique but stuck in a routine.

Appreciate school today. That two-week shutdown? Try three months of online schooling. Three months of staring at screens, watching teachers try desperately to hold onto their students' attention. Three months of canceled performances. Three months of promising to give anything—anything—for one more biology lab, one more fire drill, one more anything.

Give all your friends one last hug. Squeeze them with extra love, hold on to them a second too long. Remember the feeling of embracing someone who isn't mom, high-fiving someone who isn't your brother. Cherish little moments, giggling while buying your favorite turkey sandwich, giving your best friend a shove when she teases you. There's no guarantee you'll be able to do this again.

Resentment will brew in you: at this pandemic, the presidential response, fellow high schoolers. Watching the White House mishandle this epidemic will make you loathe our government, count down the days until the election, and wish you could vote. You'll get mad at this virus for disrupting sophomore year, costing so many American lives, keeping you awake at night, worrying about Grandpa, who had heart surgery. You'll give anything to turn back time because your entire worldview will become more judgmental.

Despite everything, don't despair. From beating Rainbow Road on Mario Kart to successful homemade croissants, your quarantine will be filled with happy memories. It'll be peppered with sad ones, too: the cancellation of summer camp will be difficult to stomach, and losing family dinners at Grandma's house will cast a shadow over Sunday nights. Perspective is key. Bond with your brother, practice piano for ten minutes longer: take all possible victories. Dad's laugh during family movie night will bring inexplicable happiness, walks with mom will make 7 a.m. exciting, losing to your brother in basketball will be bearable; you'll make priceless memories with the people closest to you.

Until now, your life has been rushing, busy. Take time to relax, and enjoy the ride. You'll be surprised at how much joy you can find in simple things if you stop and breathe.

Stay safe,
Present-day Lauren

Excerpt from "Lucid Dreams" by Jiwoo Bae, 14, Secaucus, New Jersey

Sometimes, I wonder what would have happened if Covid-19 didn't strike America. Would I have had a great end of eighth grade with a ceremony and a barbecue? Would I have had a great time with friends celebrating the end of our middle school days, knowing a lot of us would part ways? Would I have been able to confess something to a certain someone? Would I have grown closer to some friends instead of growing further away from them?

Excerpt from "A Recap" by Sofia Palomino, 16, Miami Lakes, Florida

I had a calendar since the beginning of the school year where I wrote all of my assignments. After March 13th, everything was blank.

This is a summary of my new life—the new things we had to use, the new essentials for school, the apps that helped me survive, the services that got my family through quarantine, and the new hobbies I picked up.

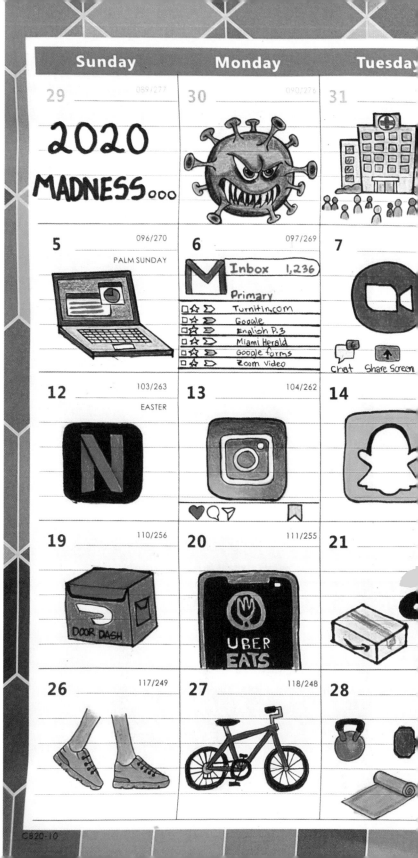

"Until Tomorrow" by Tienne Yu, 16, Freehold, New Jersey

We started the year off with a bang. Anticipant and eager, we watched the ball drop, signaling the advent of a new, fruitful decade. Then the Covid-19 virus, once an overseas news story looming at bay, hit us with full force. Caught up in the chaos of it all, everything felt like a blur: schools were closing down, new regulations were being put in place, and people were stocking up on canned food and toilet paper as if there would be no tomorrow. But there was a tomorrow, and a tomorrow after that, and then another tomorrow after that.

Now, if you can, reread this paragraph with the music playing.

I wrote "Until Tomorrow" to be a direct representation of how this past year has gone. It starts off with a cluster of melodies and voices weaving in and out. As a classical musician, these voices, of my peers, teachers, and mentors, are the most important things to me. A large part of classical music is performance and personal work, but an even larger part—what makes it the best thing in the world—is the collaboration.

The piece progresses by slowly losing its multiple voices; even when multiple voices are involved, they speak from different places at different times. I end the piece with a melody from a single voice.

Even though every inch of me is telling me to look forward and make the best of every situation, I still yearn for a time when I don't have to share my music through a screen.

See the video at https://www.youtube.com/watch?v=HofbijkSp7Y

Until Tomorrow

for solo violin

Tienne Yu

> cAn yoU PleASe StOp THerE whiLE I waLk bY?

Guide to Avoiding Awkward Social Distancing Moments

Whether you're here to learn more about ways to manage social distancing, or if you're just here to explore, welcome! After/while reading, I encourage you to think of other ways you can avoid these terrible, nerve-wracking, and often embarrassing moments so that you can become the most amazing social distancer ever!

SIDEWALK:

You are on a narrow sidewalk, taking a walk after being inside all day. A few feet ahead of you, there is another person coming towards you. You would usually be calm but careful while walking by, except: this person isn't wearing a mask. What do you do now? Well, you have three options.

1. Back into someone's driveway or front yard and wait for the person to walk by. Yes, it's technically trespassing, but we're in a pandemic, so honestly, we gotta do what we gotta do.

2. Make yourself as skinny as possible, sucking in your stomach and holding your breath to squeeze by the person. Obviously, this isn't a very safe option, but sometimes it's the only option if you don't have a corner nearby to scooch into.

3. This one is slightly safer than the second one. However, it is far more embarrassing; yell "cAn yoU PleASe StOp THerE whiLE I waLK bY?" Sometimes they listen and sometimes they don't. Of course, this is the opposite of avoiding awkward social distancing moments, but if you're comfortable doing this third one, you have my utmost respect.

DISTANCING

"For a generation, it was a
defining collective experience."

"Trapped" by Ryan Daniel, 18, Dallas

This piece, a picture I sketched of my little sister inside a box I created, depicts the entrapment and isolation felt by so many people during quarantine. This is the new normal for my generation. But we have grown together and are now capable of deeply connecting through shared experience.

"Life of a Teenage Girl 2020"
by Julia Brahms, 17, South Portland, Maine

I'm a senior in this strange time, separated from my girlfriend, friends, and the outside world. Small items in the background of the image show the protests taking place, events being canceled, hobbies I picked up during quarantine, and the messiness that's created by depressive episodes that can be triggered by isolation.

I drew this series in mid-April while sitting silently on many Zoom calls. In quarantine, my interactions with other people all fit neatly into little rectangles on my screen.

Being young is about stretching and growing. We pull away from our parents, our homes, our schools, but as Covid-19 struck our communities we were reined in to all the situations that youth is about diverging from. For some, it was a time of reflection. For many, it was a dark period of isolation. For a generation, it was a defining collective experience.

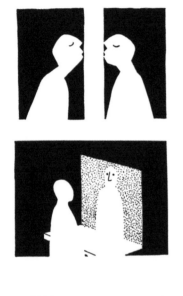

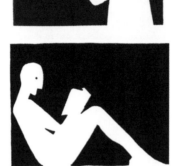

"Mask of Madness" by Annika Lachica, 14, Secaucus, New Jersey

I thought that one of the best ways to represent being a teenager during 2020 was to directly use a teenager—a.k.a. me.

Everywhere you look, everyone has a face covering on themselves. A simple piece of cloth over our mouths and noses is a foreign idea that has become the new social norm. The mask also represents a feeling of suffocation. We've all gotten so used to feeling dejected and alone that it's become the new standard.

Being isolated from the rest of the world means we're all going to have to relearn to communicate and open up with each other again.

"Lonesome Times" by Sean Patton, 14, Manhattan Beach, California

Looking down at our feet while the rain pours on our heads this year, we have no umbrella to keep us warm and protected.

"The Deck of Thoughts" by Hannah Blue, 17, Dallas

I was angry at the world and I wanted to channel my feelings into something meaningful. I chose to design my own mini deck of tarot cards. The Hermit is the only one that is actually a real tarot card; I made the other three up. I am slightly grateful to the pandemic. I feel as though I was forced to be alone with myself, with my thoughts and feelings, which led me to create art and poetry with deeper meaning than I had ever been able to create before.

"My Wall" by Ashley Renselaer, 15, Mar Vista, California

if i am not speaking
i am mute
"Young lady, hello?
Can you hear me?
Please unmute yourself.
Are you there?"
this is my wall speaking
i have four of them
they are arranged in a cube
correction: I have six of them
a ceiling is a wall
so is the floor
walls are tools of entrapment
occasionally they snuggle
but they don't procreate
having a tree sprout from the floor
of my room freeing its
branches through the panes
of my windows
would summon the cops to our front door
the fall of the Berlin Wall happened by mistake
an East German important man misspoke
then the wall fell
this is a fun fact
around 200 East Germans were killed trying to climb
    the wall and escape to West Berlin
this is not a fun fact.
this is just a fact.
my walls are envious
no one climbs them
in any direction
what is beyond them
isn't worth
death
walls are canvases
Reflections
cave painting of animals (bulls and bisons) at Lascaux
    are 17000 years old and were discovered by an
    18-year-old and his dog in 1940
i have an instagram wall
with no doors or windows and no bulls
instagram is a wall to like and comment
the instagram photo with the most likes is an egg on
    a white background

i looked for it and liked it
i didn't comment
in my country
a petty coward
became king
promising a
wall
the Great Wall of China is more than 2,300 years old and
    more than 13,170 miles long.
my room is 14 feet by 17 feet
so if I line up my four walls in a straight row, I will have a 64
    foot wall
and no room
passing our neighbor Mr. Oliver
the founder of Zen Buddhism, Bodhidharma, is said to have
    gained enlightenment by facing a wall for nine years and
    not speaking
that might be why I am mute
staring at my wall

"Distant" by Vincenzo Scicchitano, Freeport, Maine

This piece is not subtle. Not remotely. That is exactly the point.

The past year has been one of distance—social, emotional, mental, and of course, physical. The concrete, limited nature of pixel art appealed to me to show the wedge between us—omnipresent, with no end in sight.

"Restless" by Ronan Cunicelli, 16, Rose Valley, Pennsylvania

I took this picture in the living room of my house, somewhere I spent a lot of time during the four months of a stay-at-home order in my state. I was constantly pacing around, looking out the window, and trying to find anything to do with my time.

I never knew how frustrating being forced to stay inside my own house was until now.

"Seven Months at This Berry Blue Desk" by Edith Gollub, 17, Palo Alto, California

Sitting with my legs up, in a pastel chair.
My choir directors watch me sitting at this desk,
A hand pressed to my stomach,
The practice track in my ear.
They put my box next to fifty others
And try to make us blend, make us a choir.
My advisor looks at me in my pastel chair,
Reminds me to fill out this form, check on my letters of rec.
I write my college apps at this desk.
My friends watch me at this berry blue desk,
Rolling colorful dice and cheering, talking in a grand accent,
Playing a character in a world
Where they can hug their friends and fight their enemies.
We're not sitting around a table with snacks and a battle map,
But we can pretend.
I sit in my emerald prom dress at my desk,
Laughing with friends over a call.

"At least we still have senior year,"
A reassurance that dies as the months pass by.
I sit at this desk and sob,
Sob as I watch a Black man plead for his life with a knee on
   his neck,
Watch protesters be shot with rubber bullets,
Poisoned with tear gas, I am enraged at this desk.
I am at my berry blue desk with a teacher in my ear
Glancing out my window every few minutes
At the burnt orange sky and my apocalyptic backyard.
It is at my berry blue desk that I hear of false promises,
Of lies, of another death.
Seven months I have lived at this desk,
Sitting with my legs up, in a pastel chair,
Wondering just how much more of my life will pass
Staring at berry blue.

See the video at https://www.youtube.com/watch?v=fNoIRjwBG9s

MISSING WHAT MIGHT HAVE BEEN

"All those mornings waking up at 3:30 a.m. to practice, thrown out like it was nothing."

"A Certain Grief" by Sara Jarecke, 17, Lakewood, Ohio

Halloween 2020 will be on a Saturday. Senior year, Saturday night, full moon—it'll be the most fun we've had in our lives! A first of last hurrahs.

I already know none of this will happen, but I try. I plan for three friends to come over, a perfect amount for six-foot spacing. I double mask. I purchase *It* on Amazon Prime. I make cupcakes with green frosting and little eyeballs.

My sister asks my mom to take her temperature.

"Take it again," I say, over and over. Thirty more minutes. Twenty. Fifteen.

"Cancel it," my dad says.

Now, I sit in my bedroom staring at a freshly opened bag of fun size Skittles. I stare out the window at a horrendously beautiful evening.

A tray of one-eyed cupcakes sits on the table, untouched.

I feel like I could be a movie character who puts their fist through a wall. I feel like I could cry at how angry I am, but I don't. For Halloween 2020, I dress up as a runner. My neighbor asks me why I'm wearing shorts and a tank top in forty degree weather, and I decide not to tell him that it's the only way I can stamp out the fiery anger that I feel.

I run to forget that another precious memory was stolen right from my fingers.

I run to forget the sadness that's getting harder to push down, down, down into the pit of my stomach. Memory after memory has vanished—a seventeenth birthday, a spring musical, a summer performance, the last first day of school. Halloween. This time, it's different. I feel like a child with a brand new toy, only to watch it be destroyed before it could be played with. There's no warning this time, no email saying that "Unfortunately, due to Covid-19, it would be in our best interests to cancel . . ."

What would I be doing right now? My lungs ache from the cold, but I keep running. What memories are ticking by without me?

Questions burn in my mind.

How do we begin to cherish our last days of youth if we don't know how many we're going to get?

How do we accept the memories and experiences and nostalgia that we lost if we don't know what we still have to lose?

How do we face a daunting future of being grown up when we're stuck in a blurred line between youth and adulthood?

I want to scream and ask "Where can I find the time to be a teenage girl?" but a voice in the back of my head whispers back, "How do you know your time isn't already over?"

"It's Not the Same Anymore" by Thomas Zhang, 15, New York City

Basketball after school,
The sound of the dribbling basketball
On the ground.
The shouts of "I got him!"
And "Watch out, pick left!"
The cheers of victory

And the "Good games"
After a hard won game
Those were the times.
Now,
The sounds are in my mind
As I dribble the ball,

Alone.
It is not the same anymore.
Pretending to pass the ball,
Going in for a lay-up,
Dodging imaginary people.
It is not the same anymore.

"What Might Have Been"
by James Lynch, 17, West Hartford, Connecticut

Your season ending always hurts a true competitor. Your season ending when it's completely out of your control drives a true competitor crazy. Having hours upon hours of nothing to do except think about what might have been, or what memories could have been made, drives a true competitor insane.

All those mornings waking up at 3:30 a.m. to practice, thrown out like it was nothing.

This experience showed me that there are no guarantees in life. It makes me look back on the moments with my brothers that I was lucky to call teammates. Over quarantine I wanted to go back and just sit in the locker room after practice. Instead of nagging the goalie (who I'm hugging in this picture and who I carpool with) and saying, "Hurry up! I'm trying to get home!" I would sit there and realize I won't ever get to go back and have this time, with these people, in that space, ever again.

If I do get to have my senior season, I definitely won't make the mistake of taking it for granted.

(Photos by Michael Moskal)

"Musings of a Quarantined High Schooler" by Jeffrey Tan, 14, New York City

Day 1: Pitter-Patter. Pitter-Patter. The sound of rain is all I hear, drowning out the sound of my basketball. The bitter wind on my face is all I feel, as my hands grow numb from being out in the cold so long. But I grit my teeth and suck it up, as my desire to play basketball far outweighs my resentment of this weather. There's no one in sight; just me and the deserted basketball court. There's not even a hoop attached to the backboard because of de Blasio's social distancing rule.

Day 2: I'm here again. As I look around me, I think of a time when these courts were filled, when basketball was a way for me to socialize. Vivid images of my friends chest-bumping after a game-winning shot still linger in my head. But now, the basketball court has transformed into my private oasis, somewhere to escape the chaos of everyone in my apartment and the piles of homework from online schooling.

Day 3: It's raining again, but who cares? Amid my grandmother's complaints, I go outside. The rain beating at my brow, I reminisce about scoring my last points of the year. Nice shot Jeffrey! So it took you 15 minutes to finally score? Good work, freshman. But now the echoes of my friends have been replaced by the sound of rain. It's crazy how something that happened so recently feels so nostalgic.

"Happy Birthday" by Brianna Hernandez, 15, New York City

I usually spend my birthday celebrating with family and friends. This year I spent my birthday alone, speaking to my family and friends through a computer screen.

"Driving to Nowhere" by Riley Simon, 17, Freeport, Maine

I scooch off the sticky leather seat and tap my feet to the pavement ever so slowly. I scrub my palms down the sides of my pants leaving an unpleasant damp spot and feel the sweat beading on my furrowed brow. Darn, I think, sweat stains don't really shout confidence. I turn to close the door but catch a glimpse of myself in the rearview mirror.

"Mask!" my mom chirps from the passenger seat.

"Right." I pause for a moment, staring at my flushed cheeks intently in the mirror. Seeing my bare face in public almost feels like being naked.

I reach into the car and grab my mask from the unnecessary stockpile of flower-printed masks in the center console.

"You've bought way too many masks, mom," I say with a little quiver in my voice. She smiles and then gives me one of those mom looks. I guess I'm that transparent. No use in stalling though, I've got to face this at some point before 1:15 p.m.

I slam the car door a little too hard and shuffle across the DMV parking lot to a crusty looking man with a mask on that he's worn a few too many times without washing.

After that, it's all just a blur of right-hand turns, reverses, stoplights, the crusty DMV guy coughing into his elbow, and me passive-aggressively rolling his window down.

Now I find myself plopped on my bedroom floor. It's 1 a.m., I should be sleeping, but instead, I'm sprawled out on my uneven wooden floorboards delicately folding and unfolding the chalky strip of paper that caused me so much stress and anxiety.

Wow, I think. I've been wanting this since I turned my backyard into a mud pit with my Barbie Jeep. I guess it's a pretty big milestone, a defining moment of being 16, but it doesn't feel quite like that. I don't know what I expected. Maybe to feel some wave of independence and to see life from the new lens of a *licensed driver*. Instead, I'm just sitting in my room, trying to muster a single feeling of achievement or excitement.

I'm ready. I'm ready to finally understand what it's all about, what it's like to discover who I am as I gain every little piece of my independence. I'm ready to speed off and blast the radio in my 2005 SUV that leaks from the ceiling and boasts a permanent engine light. But as I look down at my mask crumpled on the floor, my open laptop displaying an assignment due an hour ago, and my unused soccer cleats tucked away in the corner, I realize I have nowhere to go.

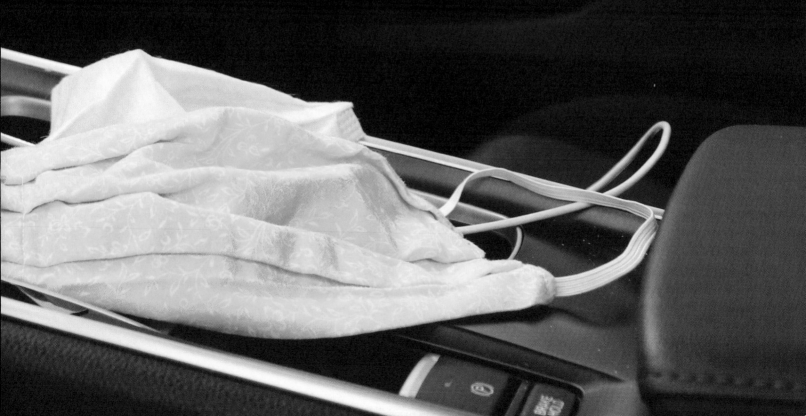

"Driver's Essentials" by Emma McIntosh, 17, San Diego

As a new driver, deciding what to keep in your car holds a unique sense of excitement and importance.

When I first began driving, I stocked my car with air fresheners, water, jumper cables, and a few other essentials.

This year there were some new additions for my destination-less drives: face masks, gloves, and extra hand sanitizer.

Imagine having something you love doing taken away from you. This is what happened to me when Covid-19 struck.

Basketball—my sport, my hobby, my escape—was locked away. Sliding my feet into a pair of white Lebrons and playing with my teammates soon became a distant memory from the past.

FEELING OVERWHELMED

"I cling to positivity, my friends,
and chewing ten packs of mint gum a day."

Excerpt from "My Boring Experience with Boredom Quarantine Journal" by Mathilde Bride, 16, Cupertino, California

As a 16-year-old, it was hard to continue school at home and be responsible for so much self-learning. To not have human contact with friends or even classmates was also a struggle because the only thoughts and opinions that I had were my own.

The judgment I imposed on myself was so much more painful than that of experiences with mean or ignorant kids from school. I was lonely, despite being surrounded by the four other people in my family.

"The Great Wave Circa 2020" by Kayla Bliven, 17, Fort Wayne, Indiana

2020 was a flood of news. I took this famous painting by the Japanese artist Hokusai and made it my own. It represents the turmoil that filled the year and acted as a bridge of shared humanity during these trying times.

"Dialogue: The Struggle to Be Productive" by Larry Witt, 18, El Cajon, California

wakes up

Larry: What should I do now, it's um . . . 2 p.m.

Brain: We have a lot of work to do but I think we can sleep for another hour.

2 hours later

Larry: It's 4 p.m. now, I slept a little too much. I should probably get some work done now.

Brain: You could get work done, but you have a whole 8 hours to do it. You just woke up, let's play some games.

3 hours later

Larry: It's getting late, I should probably do something.

Brain: You're right. Let's play some chess, since it's not going to take too long, and then get to work.

30 minutes later

Larry: We did that for too long, what assignment should I do first?

Brain: I know there's a bunch of work but I think the most important thing is to get some food right now.

Larry: I am pretty hungry, let's make food.

30 minutes later

Larry: Alright, homework time.

Brain: But . . . first we should take a shower just to feel better.

another 30 minutes later

Larry: Alright I've pulled up the assignment, let's do some work.

Brain: We've pulled up the assignment, that's enough work for now. Let's watch a YouTube video before we start.

1 hour later

Larry: It's 9:30 and I have a lot of assignments, I don't think I can finish them now so let's just do the most important ones.

Brain: You already can't finish them so let's just watch YouTube for another 30 and you can finish the last two.

Larry: Hmmm, OK.

30 minutes later

Larry: It's 10, I have time for 2 assignments.

1 hour and 40 minutes later

Larry: This assignment took way longer than normal, I won't be able to finish the second one.

Brain: You're right but we did finish one so that's better than nothing.

Larry: Maybe we should do some of tomorrow's work so it doesn't happen again.

Brain: You're right but we have all of tomorrow to do it. It's not like we'd do the same thing twice, right?

end

☆ Corona Schedule ☆

- [ ] Wake up at a random time → forget to take medication
- [ ] Eat "for the first time in hours" ???
- [ ] Zoom classes
- [ ] complain about zoom classes
- [ ] zoom classes
- [ ] zoom classes, they never end.
- [ ] Afternoon break to complain about zoom classes (2pm)
- [ ] zoom classes } lose mind somewhere
- [ ] zoom classes } here.
- [ ] lie in bed due to exhaustion due to zoom classes
- [ ] ~~sit eat text~~ Isolate from friends.
- [ ] panic attack #1
- [ ] eat cut up fruit that my mom brought me because I was sad
- [ ] waste away on social media
- [ ] panic attack #2 about the state of the world → election protests, covid, shut down
- [ ] do homework → never ending
- [ ] ~~quit~~ doing homework
- [ ] forget to eat dinner
- [ ] cry ← squeeze in headache
- [ ] cry
- [ ] try and sleep
- [ ] fail and cry

"Schedule of Monotony (or some resemblance of a schedule)"
by Chloe Rambo, 16, El Cajon, California

Before Covid hit, I was an extremely busy teenager. I didn't realize how much I relied on that to keep myself sane.

As we got deeper and deeper into quarantine, I started losing my concept of time. My mental health was at an all-time low. I felt so alone. I let go of myself. I had to start making a schedule for myself again, one I have lived every day since about August. I am so excited for life to go back to normal, but for now I have to adapt like everyone else.

"The Happenings Outside"
by Emily Milligan, 14, Reed Point, Montana

During quarantine, I had no control over what was happening. I continued with life while the world seemed to be burning. ▼

Excerpt from "2:38 p.m." by Evelyn Garcia, 15, Grapevine, Texas

I used to run at 2:38 p.m. every day.

It was a fact of life I dreaded.

But I had my friends to warm up with and run with and be sore with. I had my family to tell exaggerated, lengthy tales of my daily suffering. I had my coaches to celebrate improving times with.

As much as I sometimes loathed it, running was fun. More than that, running was a part of me, as simple as the fact that I have brown hair, that I'm 5'5", that I have a younger brother and an older sister and a gray and white cat.

Then Covid-19 arrived.

At first, we celebrated the extra two weeks of spring break on our group chats; my phone pinged constantly with new messages. But as those two weeks went by, the revelry trickled out. The contact between my friends and I grew faded and distant—a random joke, a bland response two days later. We were lost, unable to text in the carefree way we used to.

We couldn't, not when the world looked the way it did. Before us, adults scrambled, struggling to take action as over a million died. The world was imploding and we hadn't even reached the ripe age of 15.

As a kid, you think adults have all the answers. Or, the important ones at least. But when no one could agree whether or not to wear masks, I realized: they don't.

It was terrifying.

I wanted my friends. I wanted school. I wanted something. Something normal.

Anything. Anything at all.

So at 2:38 p.m., I laced up my black Nikes.

And I ran.

"TOO MUCH" by Ana Cordero, 14, Locust Valley, New York

At first, "BREAKING NEWS" every week was a bit entertaining and exciting. But after seeing how the year is going downhill, and how every bit of "BREAKING NEWS" was worse than the last, I started to get stressed. I didn't get enough time to take some things in. The news kept coming and coming.

"We Didn't Start the Virus" by Ethan Perrin, 13, Osprey, Florida

To be sung to the tune of "We Didn't Start the Fire" by Billy Joel

Kamala Harris, Mike Pence, Covid China, Donald Trump, impeachment, Joe Biden, presidential race

Giuliani, Chadwick Boseman, assaults, Protesting Republicans, Democrats, Breonna Taylor

George Floyd, second wave, drone strike, one million cases, masks, stock market crash and Dow Industrial down

Coronavirus, vaccine, Australian wildfires, pandemic, Washington, Lebanon goodbye

We didn't start the virus It was always burning Since the world's been turning We didn't start the virus No we didn't light it But we tried to fight it

Vladimir Putin, more years, Henry and Meghan, Russian voters, Maxwell, cyber attacks

Bill Gates, William Barr, Ghebreyesus, Hidalgo, Tsai Ing-wen rises, four million cases

Oil prices, cyclones, Houston's got a cheating team, tropical storms, Peter Pan, Twitter hacked, Disneyworld

Lockdown, quarantine, Italy, earthquakes Nancy Pelosi, warm weather, trouble on Twitter

We didn't start the virus It was always burning Since the world's been turning We didn't start the virus No we didn't light it But we tried to fight it

Leap year, Thailand, Jeffrey Epstein, protests, death toll, Poland abortion, Russian emergency

Royal family, Queen Elizabeth, Prince Harry stepping down, locust swarms, Iran missiles, Lebanon government

Puerto Rico, dirty water, online schooling, mafia, dam burst, dust storm, WWIII is a no-go

Flooding, earthquakes, Pence and Trump murder hornets, budgets, Russians in Afghanistan

We didn't start the virus It was always burning Since the world's been turning We didn't start the virus No we didn't light it But we tried to fight it

Weinstein, Warren, UK left the EU, stimulus, Golden Girls, Economy down the drain

White supremacists, Iowa's bad caucus, Aunt Jemima, John Roberts, Biden beats Donald Trump

Police, Splash Mountain, Ruth Bader Ginsburg's death, Kobe Bryant, blown away, what else do I have to say

We didn't start the virus It was always burning Since the world's been turning We didn't start the virus No we didn't light it But we tried to fight it

Abortion, Kim Jong Un, Joe Biden back again, Hong Kong, flash floods, missionary, Kabul, Islam, Jinping, airlines, terror on Flight 752, hornets in America, Russians in Afghanistan

"Jeopardy," Alex Trebek, online school, Zoom time, American debt, false news, BLM, census, Bernie Sanders, pets dead on the shores, forty-seven million cases, violence in Africa, I can't take it anymore

We didn't start the virus It was always burning Since the world's been turning We didn't start the virus But when we are gone Will it still burn on, and on, and on, and on

We didn't start the virus It was always burning Since the world's been turning We didn't start the virus No we didn't light it But we tried to fight it

We didn't start the virus It was always burning Since the world's been turning We didn't start the virus No we didn't light it But we tried to fight it

"A Day in the Very Ordinary Life of the Very Ordinary Aaron"
by Aaron Chen, 13, Katy, Texas

I spring up and spin around. My fingers wrap around my pillowcase, as I sniff for the stench of sweat. The overwhelming musty odor gloriously fills my nostrils. I leap down from my perch into my mountain of pillows, run to my bathroom, and force the last dollops from the tube of Colgate onto my Barney the Purple Dinosaur Limited Edition toothbrush. The painful minty mush touches my tongue. My senses are spry. Covid will not kill me today, but, on the inside, I'm already dying.

Logging into Zoom, I rub away the eye boogers to pass the time in the waiting room. Maintaining a healthy social life before quarantine was not easy, but socializing in my Geometry Zoom calls? Impossible. It is like comparing "Mary Had a Little Lamb" to Beethoven's "Hammerklavier." Within a month, quarantine had sucked my society-deprived mind into spending hours scrolling through pictures of influencers who look like Barbie dolls and recycled memes. It makes me want to die.

During lunch break, I scroll down my Instagram feed, slurping down noodles. Everyone brags that "Quarantine has made our family closer." That is impossible with my family. Before quarantine, we didn't see each other on weekdays until late afternoon. It was perfect. Once quarantine started, my sister and I started having arguments, quarrels, full-on WWE Wrestle Mania Steel Cage fights to the death. Our mood affected our parents. By the end of the day, everyone is irritable. I'm afraid if I stay inside, my family will slaughter me when I least expect it.

All these hours in front of a screen take a toll. By 9:00 p.m., the words I sputter out are a kindergartener's art project: randomly stuck together without rhyme or reason. My brain has become slush worthy of the creator of ICEE. However, my hands can still endure a few more hours of carpal tunnel thanks to my spring training in Minecraft and Pong.

I cling to positivity, my friends, and chewing ten packs of mint gum a day. What will happen if Trump fails to find a vaccine? Will all graduations, birthday parties, festivals, World Series, World Cups, Olympics, NBA Finals, Stanley Cups, and, dare I say it, Super Bowls be canceled? Not if you wear a simple cloth across your air holes. I don't give an axolotl's bare butt if you can't breathe. Doctors fight to save lives, working under pressure for long hours, all while donning PPE, and you refuse to mask up when you order your Grande Caramel Macchiato? These thoughts race through my mind as I climb the ladder to my bed and fall into a fitful sleep, dreaming of a quarantine-free world.

APPROACHING A BREAKING POINT

"I had so many feelings. Fear, anxiety, sadness, loneliness. It was like they just took turns and looped from one to the next."

"overtaxed" by Stevia Ndoe, 18, Chicago ▲

Ever since I was a child, I looked forward to my 18th birthday. I thought I would suddenly gain years of knowledge and have the power to change the world. Little did I know how difficult the year of my retirement from childhood would be.

When murmurs of quarantining were becoming a reality, my family and I were stuck. My mom, an essential worker and single parent, worked all day while my younger siblings and I attended school. On top of trying to graduate from high school, I had to be a mother for a preschooler and a grade-schooler. My 18th birthday came and went, and I was still the same Stevia.

I look at the last few months and realize this is what growing up in a global crisis looks like for low-income families. Being in quarantine made me realize how much I have been robbed of my childhood and that I've been an "adult" for the majority of my life. My photo represents waking up daily with the stress of not knowing what life is going to throw at you, but going through the motions anyway. I took this photo one morning as my siblings were still sleeping four feet away from me. The light was coming through the window so beautifully, and it was one of the few moments of silence I had experienced since March.

Excerpt from "My Emotions as Meaningless Drawings" by Madelyn Boman, 16, Juneau, Alaska

I have learned a lot about myself this year. During our Covid-19 social distancing period I had no patience or real inspiration for art, which was incredibly frustrating to me. I found the only things I had patience for were small doodles and quotes. I had an incredibly hard time this spring. These journals were my biggest outlet for processing emotions.

These sketchbooks are full of some of my more personal and raw feelings that before today I would never have been willing to share. But this year I've begun to realize that none of us are as stable as we think we are. ▼

"Super Power to Super Weakness" by Eric Hanscom, 17, Marblehead, Massachusetts

Like many adolescents, I was an excellent sleeper. Not only could I rest for seemingly limitless hours, but also program myself to wake up at a certain time. I scoffed at alarms thinking I had the superhuman ability to choose the time I wished to wake. If I had something planned and needed to wake up at 8 o'clock for it, I would just wake up at 8 on the dot. But now that the pandemic has struck, I can no longer even fall asleep.

As I lie in bed, my mind races: "Am I going to find a new job?" "Will I go back to school?" "What about college?" "Will there still be theater at the high school?" "Is my Dad going to be able to reopen his business?" "Can I count on anything anymore?"

To say I am anxious is an understatement; I am in my senior year, the year in which change is already occurring in every aspect of my life. The only things I thought I could rely on, school and theater, have ceased and I have been forced to find a new job.

After dozens of sleepless nights, I ordered melatonin pills on Amazon. I now take 12 milligrams of melatonin every night just so I can escape the unnerving thoughts that plague my mind. Still, I will occasionally wake up in the dead of night and just lie there so tired that I'm unable to sleep. Eventually, I'll fall back to sleep, but once day breaks I either start my day or collapse deeper into my mattress, wide awake, questioning everything.

Sometimes I feel more like an old man on the verge of retiring rather than an up-and-coming youth on the march towards life.

"Isolation Thoughts" by Jayda Murray, 16, Millington, Tennessee

From a young age, I looked at the world from the lens of a dreamer. Flame-colored sunlight would dance through windows, and water would trickle below trees. I created scenes in my head until I found that a pen and paintbrush could do the same. I wanted those pictures and worlds to have substance in reality. That same inspiration drives my creative process as a teenager.

Before Covid-19 hit our American shores, I felt an increasing sense of dread. Two weeks later, my county issued a lockdown, and all my friends either found themselves at home or were recklessly disobeying the order. I had so many feelings. Fear, anxiety, sadness, loneliness. It was like they just took turns and looped from one to the next.

"Artist's Block" by Bella Muñoz, 16, San Antonio, Texas

Being constantly surrounded by the same walls for a matter of months, I began to suffer every artist's worst fear—artist's block.

With the lack of inspiration came a lack of drive, and I soon became heavily entrenched in the world of social media. Instagram, YouTube, and Tumblr became my daily routine, and my emotional state deteriorated significantly.

Nothing made me happy anymore, all I wanted was to shut my eyes and wake up in 2021.

"field hockey, the future, and my emotional roller coaster: an unedited journal entry" by Natasha Ring, 16, Wilton, Connecticut

Right now, I'm supposed to be at field hockey tryouts. Instead, I'm in bed crying. Field hockey's postponed and I might have corona. I want to scream and cry and punch something.

5:30 our schedule was released, 5:38 they emailed saying practice was canceled, and 5:41 a Facebook post from the captains told us why. It's just past 6 now, and I'm still in shock.

Our world is upside down. I saw friends for the first time since March 11, who I used to see daily. California is burning and looks like Mars with the pumpkin orange sky, and 3 days a week I'm doing school from my bedroom. Nothing is the same. I haven't left the county since March, or met my cousin who was born in June and lives an hour away.

When Grandpa was in high school, he played football in the fall, baseball in the spring, and had 3 hours of homework a night. That was just 45 years ago. Now I'm trying to balance year-round field hockey, rowing, 5–6 hours of homework a night, working out, drivers ed, college searches, and a global pandemic. It's no wonder teenagers are so stressed! Freshman year in my humanities class of 46 kids, the vast majority reported not getting enough sleep, forgetting meals, and having many hours of homework every night. We were only 14.

Now I wonder if I've hit my breaking point. There's so many unknowns and everything changes so fast. 24 hours from now will I be the same person I was when I woke up this morning?

"I'm Fine" by Reagan Henderlite, 14, Cornelius, North Carolina

"I'm fine." The lie easily slips past our lips after rehearsing the sentence over and over. Our generation doesn't want others to carry our burdens, so we keep our problems to ourselves. We don't want to be the reason that someone else feels the same way we do.

Or maybe it's because we don't trust you with our honesty. Maybe it's because, when we do tell the truth, our small cries for help fall on deaf ears. "Attention-seeking," "immature," "dramatic," "complaining," "overreacting"—any effort made to explain ourselves is ignored and excused.

Adults don't understand that we are lost and drowning in this world where we are expected to carry so much weight. One would be foolish to believe that the backbone of an entire generation could be upheld by two little words.

"Just Breathe" by Sunnina Chen, 16, Whippany Park, New Jersey

If you're reading this, take five deep breaths.

Wasn't that nice?

"Just breathe" became a mantra I told myself to get through the simple things. Taking the time to reflect, I realized why the Saran Wrap was suffocating me—I was the one who pulled it tight. Yes, it was placed there by my responsibilities and the uncertainty of our world, but I had the ability to let go. I let go of everything that wasn't serving me, and took a deep breath.

CONFRONTING ANTI-ASIAN XENOPHOBIA

"He lifted a pink finger and started shouting 'Chinese virus' and 'Go home.'"

"Am I to Blame?" by Rebecca Wong, 17, Tenafly, New Jersey

2020 didn't ignite the waves of Asian racism—it was already there.

I've seen the Asian community strive to be "more American." I saw my family disassociate themselves from the community. My dad never taught me a lick of Cantonese in hopes to make me "more American"; I know he was trying his best for us. I erased my own culture willingly in hopes of fitting in—it's always purposeful whitewashing, the strive for Americanizing in hopes to be accepted.

Though, you'll still see the person I tried to erase. I cannot wash my culture away; it will always stay—the racism will always stay.

At least paint is washable.

"When They Say You Will Never Be Clean" by Kristine Ma, 15, Beverly Hills, Michigan

it is the first time i had to ask my mom if it was safe
to go in a store alone, a fifteen-year-old chinese girl.
when you went on the bus, they asked if you were sick. your cheeks burned.
a girl who looks like you, who could be you
is bleeding in the street, her hands over her head.
they call her diseased. *dirty chinese.* an old woman on the train
in the seat next to you, attacked. you pull the hood over your head a little tighter,
cover the skin on your hands with the sleeves. you shrink until there's nothing left,
but this is my country, but this is my home, repeating it like a mantra.
it is the first time in four years that you hear his nasally voice again in your dreams,
the new york streets, his grip on your wrist, on your hips—
come on, pretty asian girl. yellow fever, they called it. a metaphorical illness.
you see news articles—people burned with acid, slashed with daggers
for their skin tone tinted a little more gold, their eyes a different shape. your heartstrings
pull when your dad asks, less than half-joking, to the air—do you think i'll get attacked
in the grocery store? when no one laughs, you shift your fork to your other hand.
your mom must explain to everyone who pries
that the chinese government is not us. the government that silences. here,
you will speak, and yet. when you were little, you prayed every night before you went to sleep
for blonde hair, blue eyes. it is the first time you wished you were white
in six years.

"Inner Conflict" by Waverly Huang, 16, State College, Pennsylvania

Who I see in the mirror is not a threat or someone who should be directly affiliated with a pandemic, but a teenager who has already felt the back-and-forth of being Chinese American and has to endure the clashing of both cultures.

These two sides of me are so different, yet they both compose my identity. I struggled, and still struggle, with figuring out if I am more like one than the other, especially in current times where it feels like the Asian part of me is less like a thing I should be proud of and more like a thing I should hide.

I never liked dumplings before March. Other Chinese foods were alright, but I think it was the blatant stereotypicality of dumplings—the slant-eyes, the dog food, the "dum-pah-ring"—that haunted me through six tearful years. I am grateful now to live in a very accepting and kind neighborhood. Yet, somewhere, sometime, I knew the stereotype lived on. So whenever my parents, these soft-spoken Chinese-American immigrants, cooked dumplings, I'd politely decline.

That changed one Saturday in March, after the inevitability of coronavirus settled in, right before the toilet paper-fueled mania started. We were waiting in Costco's checkout line, my mother watching her phone and I a nearby cereal box. Just as I was scanning the nutrition label, the box was yanked away and loaded into the cart of someone on the opposite side of the shelf. I found myself staring at the eye of a man where the calorie count used to be.

He lifted a pink finger and started shouting, "Chinese virus" and "Go home" among other things I'm too embarrassed to repeat. He threw something—hand sanitizer—across the shelf.

I froze. For ten seconds or ten minutes, I found myself stunned into the powerlessness of an eight-year-old again. It was elementary school, except the playground bullies had grown into adults and ignorance into hatred. My silence hung pathetically while the man swaggered away.

My mom tugged on my arm. "I was on the phone. Was he talking to us?" she asked in Mandarin.

"No."

Two hours later in Midland, Texas, a nineteen year-old would stab a Burmese man and his two children. When asked about his motives, he said he wanted to stop them from infecting others with the coronavirus.

"Mom, you should probably speak more English when you're in public now," I told her later that day.

She stared at me for a second. Then, in crisp Xi'an Mandarin, she told me to help her with the dumplings. She turned around and, resolution set in her brow, kept kneading.

I joined her. For the first time since I was seven, I found myself rolling flour circles, ragged from years without practice. This time, I stood taller than my mother, and this time, a tacit message passed between us. The world had degraded into elementary school, but I wouldn't degrade with it, because I was twice as old, twice as tall, twice as bold as before. I don't think I'd win if I came face-to-face with that man again. But if there is one battle I have waged and won, it is the one with my past self. It's not enough, nor is it close to enough, but it is a start. A fragrant, pork-stuffed start.

Excerpt from "Gaze" by Sangjun Um, 17, Blairstown, New Jersey

As an Asian teenager studying in America, I wanted to deal with issues of racial violence against Asians in the United States when the pandemic first struck.

Even in these difficult times, we can still find hope and unity, as long as our "masks" of prejudice are off. I believe that we can come together, barriers broken, in this fight.

"You can't stop me from going, Naomi."

I stared at my Bachan. Normally calm and sweet, she stared at me with a stern gaze. The dinner table had grown uncomfortably silent. Jichan coughed awkwardly and cleared his mouth with a sauce-covered napkin. I struggled to compose myself.

"Bachan. It's not smart to go. You're 90. You're in a high-risk population, when they tell you to stay inside, stay inside!"

Bachan waved her hand dismissively. "Naomi, it's fine. Swansons Nursery has so many protocols, and I'm not going near anyone, I just need new fertilizer! Stop worrying."

Mom and I glanced at each other. Was this a sign of my beloved grandmother becoming senile? She watched CNN nearly every waking hour of the day and yet didn't realize the risks this pandemic brought to her especially?

Mom shook her head woefully and whispered, "She's going to do it no matter what, Naoms. It's fine, let's just go home."

I smacked my head dramatically but made my way around the table to kiss Bachan and Jichan goodbye. "Stay safe," I admonished.

Bachan chuckled. "Of course I will."

On the drive home I stared out the window at the horizon, marveling at how stunning Seattle is in the spring. Japanese cherry blossoms line the streets, and on a sunny evening like that night, you might find crowds of people swarming the UW campus, clamoring for the perfect Instagram shot or Snapchat story. However, those days of large gatherings and camaraderie beneath the cherry blossoms had long since disappeared, their only remnants the hulking trees that continued their march through the seasons. While most routines of pre-Covid life had disappeared, one that remained were weekly dinners with my Mom, Bachan, and Jichan. We'd gather at their messy house in North Seattle, and for a blissful hour, forget the world outside that delved into chaos. It was during these dinners that I realized my grandmother was leaving the house more than anyone I knew. She visited Costco, QFC, Nordstrom, Fred Meyers, Swansons, and many more, all while everyone else kept inside and turned to Amazon as their strict method of purchasing. Why would she do this? Put herself at risk to load up on 24 rolls of toilet paper? Or purchase new rhododendrons for her garden? It made no sense.

I grumbled about this the whole ride home, ranting to Mom somewhat incoherently. Mom nodded along politely, but as we pulled into the garage, she posed her own theory, "Maybe she feels like she's locked up again? Like her freedoms are being taken away again, and she's trying to resist it." I stared at her, dumbfounded. Of course.

This pandemic was not the first time Bachan had been told she couldn't go places. Nearly 80 years ago, she was placed in a cage for three years, and was stripped of every liberty she should have been afforded. She and her family were loyal US citizens who were told they were the enemy due to their Japanese heritage. In the land of the free, she was given no freedoms. Every restriction imaginable was placed on her.

Now as a global pandemic swept into her life, that same weight of erased liberties settled on her shoulders. As the world shut its doors, she knocked on them, determined to maintain those rights that had previously been stripped from her unjustly. Her decisions to go out into the world at age 90 were based not in ignorance, but fear. Fear that the country that stole her freedoms was doing it once again.

ENDURING COVID-19

*"You can hear your dad
coughing through the walls."*

"okay" by Suhaylah Sirajul-Islam, 15, Brooklyn

What's it like, being a teenager in quarantine?

it's the same i guess.

except time passes more slowly.

and you're not allowed to go outside.

it's feeling exhausted from all the schoolwork.

and touch-starved because your friends aren't there.

suddenly, the two-bedroom apartment you share with five family members,

finally begins to feel cramped.

it's feeling terrified, because you share a room with your covid-positive aunt, who refuses to see a doctor.

and you can hear your dad, coughing through the walls.

and your mom at 2 a.m, reciting Qur'an and rushing to make tea for the both of them.

she gets sick too.

and suddenly you're failing classes because you can't keep up with helping your siblings, and classwork, and housework, and the sick adults at home.

things start to look up though.

the weather gets warmer.

and your family gets better.

being a teenager in quarantine,

it's feeling homesick for the mosque when Ramadan begins,

but grateful you get to spend time with family.

it's celebrating Eid in your living room, dressed in your best clothes while munching on fuska and kebabs.

and it's letting yourself grieve when May 29th comes near.

finally cleaning out your closet of her old clothes.

and it's feeling hollow, seeing all the new covid related graves around your sister's.

(it's been a year, you'll be alright.)

being a teenager in quarantine is falling ill when protests start.

you can't forget their names.

or the anger

and the pain

and a need for justice

trying to do as much as you can

it's feeling tired

of all the fevers and trips to the bathroom you've been having

it's seven hours in the hospital with your older sister by your side, while the doctors bruise your arms with IVs and stick cotton-swabs up your nose.

you test positive for covid on the very last day of school,

but hey,

at least you passed your classes.

being a teenager in quarantine,

is spending your 15th birthday eating chinese food with tastebuds you lost to covid.

it's spending July throwing up in the bathroom, watching Netflix with your siblings, writing letters to your friends in case you die, and recovering.

it's processing repressed trauma with your brother and sister in August, and hyper-fixating on Hunter X Hunter together.

in September,

it's doing your summer homework the day it's due

and missing classes because of burnout.

in October, you see a psychiatrist,

a therapist too,

you will get better.

you still miss class and hand in assignments late though.

but it's alright.

being a teenager in quarantine

is radical acceptance.

things happened and things are happening

you'll be okay.

you survived,

and you'll be okay.

"Ghosts and Kittens" by Meg Lockhart, 16, Houston

My father's ghost hovered above my shoulder less like a cohesive presence and more like a tangled skein of yarn twisted around the tears, the fights, and the tentative, guilty relief he left in his wake after he died in May. The ghost hung over my shoulder when I stepped into my Dad's room for the first time since the paramedics dragged him outside on a stretcher while he had a heart attack, which was likely related to a suspected Covid-19 case a week before. His room was cleaner than he left it, and emptier, but his shoes were still tucked under a half-finished table, his books still stacked on his nightstand, and the mattress still smelled like his urine. I'd been avoiding his room for months, but my family decided there wasn't a better place to introduce a few kittens to our house.

I tiptoed across the room as I taped cardboard from the million packages I'd received in the mail to anywhere the cats could jump out of the room or get up too high to climb down. Sweet things, one ginger and one black, and their footsteps just as light as mine. The kittens were rescues, taken from the street and now from their foster home. They trembled a bit at first; their own ghosts followed them from wherever they lived before they came to my house. I had expected this, so I turned a cardboard box into a cave for them to hide in. Toys were scattered across the floor because kittens, even haunted ones, need to play.

I sat on the abandoned bed. My work wasn't perfect, but it was good enough. I wondered briefly what my father would think: he liked cats enough but he wanted a dog. His ghost, looming, watched with cold, gentle eyes as I thumbed through a book he'd left behind.

I would be startled by how alive the kittens were, even with their ghosts following them, but we'd get used to each other and our ghosts. Their presence was peaceful, somehow, in a room filled with death.

"A Message of Hope" by Tara Suri, 14, New York City

My grandfather is 75 years old and a Covid-19 survivor.

In his early twenties, he arrived in New York with a suitcase and a few dollars. He drove a taxi cab for a living. Now he loves fixing cars, traveling, and is a very outgoing person. He has a weak heart condition that makes him stay focused on his routine of daily exercises. He has always told me the importance of working hard and staying positive.

I created this artwork when my grandfather sent me this photo in March 2020 during his stay at the hospital with Covid-19. When he went to the ER, he had to wait a long time to be admitted because there were no beds available. School had just closed and Covid-19 cases in New York were growing daily. As the days progressed, my grandfather got sicker. His oxygen levels got lower, and his lungs were very inflamed. I would FaceTime my grandfather daily. I was beginning to feel helpless.

Despite the slim odds of survival for patients in his age group, my grandfather never gave up hope. Luckily, he survived.

"Comfort" by Virginia Fowler, 16, Wilmington, North Carolina

My mom is a nurse, and the toll that her work takes has been bleeding into her home life. When she comes home my sister and I can't get near her, let alone touch her until she changes clothes and showers. She's cried to us for her patients who are trying to recover without comfort or support from loved ones because of the lockdown and visitors being banned from hospitals. I tried to show the emotional burden that hospital staff have been expected to carry throughout the course of this pandemic. ▼

"On the Line" by Jessica Wang, 16, Palo Alto, California ▲

To my dad, these sunbathing masks in our backyard are necessary. Most of the masks on this line are his—the Friday surgical mask, the biking-to-work neck gaiter, a mask for each day of the week. Rather than simply airing out, the adornments absorb ultraviolet radiation to damage any possible nefarious microbes or viruses. In essence, they're being cleansed by the sun.

They are the barriers between life and death for workers in the medical field. They are the barriers between life and death for my dad.

This snapshot represents everything that changed between my sophomore and junior year of high school. Coming of age during Covid-19, I experienced the worry, the stress, and the pride of having a parent working and risking his life on the front lines.

"I am Positive" by Victoria Iuzzolino, 18, Millstone, New Jersey

I have always been positive.
I could have failed an exam,
Missed the bus,
Or just dealing with friendship drama,
I was always looking on the bright side.
I was always positive.
That is why when the pandemic hit, I knew I had to be nothing but positive.

When the lockdowns began,
And my sister miserably was sent home from college,
I knew I needed to be positive for everyone.
I baked happily as the news rang the numbers of cases rising in my county.
I dyed shirts with my sisters while my parents whispered about "what if's?"
The what if my grandma caught the virus,
or what if we can never go back to school again.

Still, my strength to be positive surpassed those worries,
even as it seemed the world was crumbling around us.

As warmer weather hit I went to the beach and watched a new blue sea;
an ocean of blue medical masks walking in different directions.

I swam in my pool as my friends stood at the opposite end, socially distanced.
We would shout from shallow end to deep end until the legs of the swimmer in the deep gave out.
Then we switch sides.
I now sit in a parking lot.
Throat scratchy,
nose sniffly,
and body aching.

In any other scenario, this would be a common cold,
however, this was the year of Covid-19, where even a normal stuffy nose caused panic.
As I watch the doctor at the urgent care go from open car window to open car window with a nose swab, I pray.

Please, for once,
let me be negative.

"Borscht Recipe" by Daniel Rykunov, 17, New York City

Ingredients:
1 pound beef
4 potatoes
2 carrots
½ beet
½ cabbage
1 onion
1 can of tomato paste
1 bay leaf (optional)

Pour 1 gallon of water and the pound of beef into a pressure cooker.

Add salt to taste.

Boil with lid closed and locked for 30–40 minutes.

While broth is boiling, chop the onion into small pieces and cook in a pan with olive oil until transparent.

Add chopped beet and carrots to onions and cook until beets and carrots are soft.

Peel and cut potatoes into large pieces and add to pot, allow to boil for 5 minutes.

Add the beets and carrots to the pot, then add chopped cabbage to the pot.

Boil for 5–7 minutes or until cabbage becomes soft.

Add the can of tomato paste to the pot and boil for 1 minute.

Add bay leaf and serve with rye bread and garlic.

This is a recipe for borscht that I cooked in April for my dad when he was ill with Covid-19 after I recovered from it.

During this time, I had to take care of the whole family while dealing with an intense workload from my school. It was one of the scariest times in my life, because my father was close to having to go to the hospital and I was worried about losing my father two years after my mother.

In addition, my teachers were lost in how to deal with the pandemic and decided to give us more work.

Overall, this year has had some of the lowest times of my life.

"My Mother's Healing Hands" by Gabrielle Bautista, 17, Hempstead, New York

One of the things I remember when I was little was my mother's hands. I would always wonder why they were so rough and wrinkly, and I thought they were not very attractive. As I grew up, I came to understand it is because she is an extremely hard worker.

My mother is an immigrant from the Philippines who came by herself, leaving her family of 12 to come to America in the 1990s as a nurse.

My mother has been working with Covid patients daily since there is such a demand for healthcare workers during the pandemic. When she comes home from work, she isolates herself from my family.

I wanted to tell the story of her hands and the hard work behind them.

"The Colored Lenses of 2020" by Emma Kraja, 13, Brooklyn

Art has been my coping mechanism for the new chaos. 2020 has thrown everything at us, but we persevere and stand tall like statues because that is what makes us human. These four moments express my 2020 experience. The last drawing, in black and white, represents a small soul swallowed by the deafening silence of death. It offers a moment to reflect on the innocent who have had their lives stolen from them by the coronavirus.

"What a Time" by Hunter Towne, 17, Freeport, Maine

this was the year

this was my year

the year i could drive

the year of romantic flings, parties, and late nights at the beach

the year of road trips, huge concerts, and dancing all night

this was the year of the one o'clock curfew

my parents' big speech

the "we trust you, you're old enough

you can do what you like"

but a pandemic happened instead

slumber parties and beach days are replaced

by facetime calls and "social-distancing" picnics

instead of traveling, i stay inside for two months straight

my friends and i skip our years-long birthday traditions

i haven't hugged them in so long

i miss concerts and shows and my favorite cousin's wedding

i speak to my grandparents only over speakerphone as we stand by the window

i only see my whole family once

my great-grandfather dies at 101

alone for weeks in rehab because we couldn't visit him

we forgo covid restrictions for a family-only funeral

everyone tries to wear a mask, but my great-grandmother is crying too hard to wear hers

there are no hugs or comforts

once the preacher finishes his sermon, we lay a flower on the casket and drive away

there's no gathering for a meal or saying a real goodbye

we just leave before great-grandma can realize we're gone and beg us to stay

now thanksgiving and christmas are on their way

and i've yet to have the year i planned

i turn 17 this month.

God, what a time.

COPING AND REINVENTING

"We made sure this day wouldn't go to waste.
We had as much fun as we could."

"Here's to 2021" by Thomas Kauffman, 17, Lance Algabre, 17, Andrew Garcia, 17, Juneau, Alaska

We wrote this song to try and spread some positivity to teenagers all over the world. We recorded different parts at our houses. We videoed some of the instruments live and some not. All of the videoed vocals are lip synced in order to increase the workflow, creativity, and fun.

Lyrics:
I just wanna I just wanna go outside
Staying inside's got me losing my mind.
I just wanna I just wanna go outside
Staying inside's got me losing my mind.
I just wanna go outside, staying inside I've lost my mind
I think about all those times
Remember those good old days
Before we stood six feet away
Now they are just memories to play.
At the end of the day, no matter what happens,
I just want you guys to remember . . .
We'll all be okay.

See the video at https://www.youtube.com/watch?v=zVMpJG4fqm8

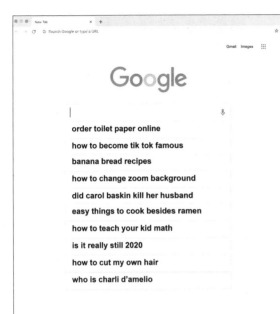

"Trending in 2020" by Piper Chase, 17, Wilton, Connecticut

There is a unique and often overlooked element that lightens the heavy load this year has thrown upon our shoulders: laughter.

Dozen of trends and new norms resulted from the bizarre time spent in "the Q."

As people across the world faced similar feelings of loneliness, fear and anxiety, we turned to technology to build and maintain social connections. Highlighting the trending memes and hilarious issues of living in quarantine created a sense of community and relief from the harsh realities outside our homes.

"Trifles" by Celine Min, 16, Bellevue, Washington

Ever since I was young, I've dreamed about grand 16th birthdays. Anything from extravagant locations to inviting hundreds of guests to even multitiered cakes. However, the reality I ended up having to face . . . my 12-year-old self would've felt crushed.

I had a small dinner with only a couple people. I came home to see a small bouquet of flowers on my dining table. After cleaning the table and placing the flowers in a vase, I noticed a stark contrast between their brightness and my surroundings. The cleaning materials were all one dull color, but the flowers were a vivid pink.

In that moment, I felt like they represented a bloom of hope.

② ANGER
There was so much hair in my eyes.

③ BARGAINING?
Not sure if this qualifies, but I was fervently wishing to be relieved of looking...

THE FIVE STAGES? FIVE STAGES OF GRIEF: QUARANTINE BANGS EDITION

① DENIAL
This expression was genuine. Truly.

④ And... DEPRESSION
Yes, my hair looks like a lumpy triangle. Wh... of it...

TR: I am completely fine... this decisi...

RECONSTRUCTION, SHOCK, THE UPWARD DISBELIEF, TURN? REFLECTION

⑤ ACCEPTANCE!

"...e Stages of Grief: Quarantine Bangs Edition" by Anushka Chakravarth...
...ound, Texas

...ut my bangs in August. It was a spur of the moment decision, but I still took the time to document it, be...
...ches of hair at the front of your face for the first time is momentous, even in a pandemic. After, I fe...
...e was a random act of teenagerishness to which no cause could be attributed, but my hair-cutting di...

...ur own hair is something of a quarantine meme at this point. Thousands of teenagers have posted...
...own (often unsuccessful) haircuts on social media. So many of us are more isolated than ever, but...
...ommunity and share in small triumphs and failures.
...e is what being a teenager is like during these times. We protest systemic injustices, mourn the lo...
...vocate for a better world. We miss our friends and understand that though everything is terrible, we...

"from my notes app, 6/2/2020 at 7:02 p.m." by Samantha Liu, 16, Basking Ridge, New Jersey

Everything feels upside down but at least there's Pepper. Even now, he curls in the same spot by my foot when I'm reading, the way he's been doing since he was five months old. For him, there's no reason to break routine. For him, all of humanity isn't spinning off its axis and hurtling towards some black, unbroken expanse. For him, he has companions in us, and that's enough to keep him happy.

I'm jealous. My companions have been reduced to ghosts, whose trails I saw today when dropping off my textbooks. There's the senior lot which burst with neon-painted cars and unhinged confidence last fall—CLASS OF 2020, BEST YEAR YET. There's the door, now locked, by which our tracksuit-clad gym teacher would stand and cheer for bleary-eyed sleep-walkers to "look alive!" There's the hallway where we mourned our chem grades, the bench where we talked to boys we liked, the entrance where we doordashed Chipotle on Thursdays, the road where we bid goodbye only to see each other the very next morning.

Apparently, that's not normal anymore. Yesterday I saw anti-mask protests on the news and thought of *The Handmaid's Tale* (because summer reading, if not Covid, will be the death of me). "We were a society dying of too much choice," said the Aunt whose name I can't remember, but whose archetype I can—the fervent, manipulative, Gilead-worshipping extremist. So, you know, when the propaganda machine starts to resound, then we've really straddled too dangerously the line between democracy and anarchy. But then again, during a massive plague, is the idea of dystopia so far-fetched?

That's what's weird. It's not the socio–politi–econo–enviro revolution itself (well, it is), but it's also the ambiguity with which we play into it. Because yeah, we're right in the middle of history, but we're also limited to playing Animal Crossing and craving chili fries while it unfolds. We're finally inside the museum display glass, but our resin-trapped hands can't touch anything. We're the side characters while the patriarchy grapples with itself and the Red Center degenerates into a brainwashing Bible camp. It's ironic. And painful. And after scrolling aimlessly through Instagram for yet another hour today, I'm also starting to think it's slightly boring. Making history is way overrated.

But we can cope. We can reject existential questions and rose-tinted memories and just embrace the new normal. Like Pepper, who is still fast asleep and will remain so until I lay out his food in one hour. He remains content, and even though he is not changing the world, that is enough for him.

So I, newly-dubbed side character, will do the same, because nothing stopped the housekeeper from baking a plate of kickass brownies while Gilead crumbled upon itself.

**"Six Feet Apart" by Paloma Ezzet, 15,
San Diego, California**

Doing common high school things, such as spending time with
your friends and going to football games, are near impossible to
do this year.

For now, we can only wait patiently.

"Homecoming 2020" by Tanner DeHaven, 18, Weston, Missouri

Students had to follow guidelines to protect themselves and others from the virus while keeping the rituals of homecoming alive. All students were required to wear masks and practice social distancing for the entirety of the parade route. In previous years, students were allowed to throw candy to the bystanders but that was retired too.

The restrictions took away an element of continuity and pride, but the spirit of homecoming was in full swing, with floats dressed in school colors and music making you want to dance with glee.

(Pictured above are a pair of candidates for their 2020 homecoming royal court)

(Photo by Michelle DeHaven)

(Photo by Catherine Modzelewski)

"Covid-19 Confirmation" by Christian Modzelewski, 14, Oceanside, New York

Church is supposed to be a place of union, a place where all peoples can get together and feel peace of mind. Sadly, my Confirmation was quite the opposite. We were forced to social distance, pews were roped off, we all needed to wear masks, including the priests, and they even blessed us with holy water via Q-tip, instead of using their hands.

In times of crisis, we can come together and celebrate something that is important to us, even if it comes with some bumps in the road.

In the custom for Jewish boys, preparation for learning to read from the Torah (Jewish Bible) begins around a year before turning 13. At your first lesson with your bar mitzvah teacher, you learn the symbols and sounds to sing when reading your parsha (weekly Torah portion). Then, it's several months of constant practice—learning the Hebrew words, learning to sing using symbols above/below the Hebrew letters, and finally learning to sing without any vowels or symbols.

Depending on the weekly portion, it can be a short one or a long one to learn. Mine was definitely in the longer category (30 minutes to sing end to end with 126 verses in 258 lines for a total of 1,932 words—not that I was counting), which I learned to recite in those weekly lessons.

For the first 6 months, weekly lessons took place at my dining room table with my teacher sitting next to me. Then, the pandemic hit. For two months, there was so much going on in the world and so much to think about, that I had simply forgotten about practicing at all and had no lessons. After that, I had two months of lessons via Zoom weekly in preparation for my big upcoming bar mitzvah date in August 2020.

As the day of my bar mitzvah was fast approaching, it became clear that this would not be a normal one like my older brother's. There were questions I never thought would have to be considered, such as could I even read my parsha inside or would it be done outside in a parking lot? Could we even have the minimum number of men required for our prayer service? How would I sing the 1,932 words wearing a mask, which reduces the breathing in the way I am usually used to singing?

My bar mitzvah was more meaningful than I expected, even during a pandemic. We had a Zoom-mitzvah celebration, Zoom prayer service with my grandfather's synagogue, and two small in-person socially distanced services, including one on my bar mitzvah day. More people joined the Zoom celebration from far away than could have joined pre-pandemic. For months, my family secretly wrote emails and letters to my favorite people, places, sports, games and foods. It was so meaningful to receive "mazal tovs" from sports teams, authors, celebrities, chefs, museums, historical sites, foods, restaurants, games, as well as from family and friends.

I am a passionate reader, so I did a contactless book drive in honor of my bar mitzvah to help families that can't buy their own books. I donated over 1,500 books to a local book foundation in New Jersey.

Turning 13 was unexpectedly amazing.

"My 2020 Graduation," by Mariam Khalil, 15, Secaucus, New Jersey

(Photo by Suzan Khalil)

"SMILE one more time! Come on, it's your graduation," mom said.

Yes, I was part of the class of 2020. Instead of being at the school's bathroom with my friends fixing ourselves before the ceremony, I graduated eighth grade online, at home, I felt trapped behind a screen. It was embarrassing. Having to stare at a camera for two hours was enough. And if you looked away, it was considered that you were not paying attention. Stress was at its highest too. You are at home, so maybe your mom walked in unintentionally. Your mic won't work, the camera is blurry.

This was my last year with my friends, and we couldn't properly spend it with each other. I couldn't hug each one of them. We couldn't take the last group photo and couldn't show off our dresses to each other. We couldn't be there to say our final goodbyes. So after we graduated online the whole class FaceTimed, cracked jokes, played games, told riddles, and watched Netflix together. We made sure this day wouldn't go to waste. We had as much fun as we could.

Knowing that I was safe, and by remaining at home it meant I saved another person's life, eased a bit of the dejection away.

(Photo by Lynn Cox)

"A Ballerina's Life in 2020" by Emilia Alioto, 13, Novato, California

Ten joyous years of dancing has made me realize that pursuing a passion is like riding a bike on a gravel road: it's bumpy and takes effort.

For nine months, I and many other dancers were trapped in our homes. Zoom was the new dance studio, ballet class was located in living rooms, and social interaction didn't exist—only a simple thumbs up or thumbs down when a teacher asked if the combination made sense. Finally, my ballet school emailed the announcement of its reopening.

In 2020 dance class looks different. All studios are outside. Big white canopies cover the dance floors and white Christmas lights are wrapped around the poles for light when it gets dark. The grass area is the replacement for locker rooms, and the outdoor benches are the new lobby. Everyone is obligated to wear a mask and stay six feet apart. It's a completely new way of life, but I would pick it over Zoom ballet any day.

"Running Toward the Season" by Kenneth DeCrosta, 18, Fairfax, Virginia

The Virginia High School League delayed all sports until December when, if it is safe, the basketball season will begin. In preparation for the start of a potential season, basketball players have been permitted to engage in physical training sessions since the beginning of October.

Players are barred from using indoor facilities; all workouts must take place outside. There are a strict set of guidelines that must be followed including online sign-ins, mandatory temperature checks, being masked at all times, sanitizing each player's personal ball, and maintaining at least six feet between each other.

Despite the restrictions, the majority of athletes from the Robinson basketball team have participated in these sessions. They have shown up faithfully, often on days when the weather has been hot and muggy, to prepare for a season that may still be canceled.

"Quarantine Workout" by Myles Gaffney, 17, Manhattan Beach, California

I have Type 1 diabetes and a number of other immune system issues. To make matters worse, my mother was just diagnosed with breast cancer. She had surgery in March the day before everything was shut down. We took it very seriously. No one other than our family was allowed in the house.

My one refuge had always been the ocean. I was on the surf team at school and we surfed five days a week at 6:30 every morning. It kept me in shape and it kept me sane. Covid shut down the surf team, then officials closed the beaches in LA county.

My dad had a bunch of nice weights in the garage that weren't getting used. We converted the garage into a home gym. The quiet alley gave us some additional space. It wasn't easy at first. I was in shape to surf, but I could barely do one pull-up.

As I started to develop some strength, I really got into it. When online school Zoom started to drag, I daydreamed about doing deadlifts and squats. I read up on physiology and kinesiology. I started eating more protein. Legs one day, chest and shoulders the next, followed by back and arms. I forced myself to rest a day or two a week, only because I knew it was necessary.

My friends wanted to come over and work out in our garage but I had to be firm. Kids in our town aren't in school, but they definitely are gathering in large groups on the weekends.

I can't say I'm not lonely. I miss hanging out with everyone. But Covid is ramping up again. I just want to stay safe, for my sake and my mom's.

CONNECTING WITH FRIENDS

"We shared little bits of ourselves with each blue-and-white text bubble."

When I decided to spend my freshman year of college at home, thousands of miles away from my peers on campus, I knew I'd have a year filled with FOMO. But I didn't anticipate how badly the loneliness would sting.

My high school friends seemed to have moved on with their lives. Meeting new people online was hard—especially the small talk. Some days, I'd lie on a sunny patch of carpet floor, utterly exhausted by Zoom. I missed feeling understood.

If I wanted to make friends, I would have to toughen up and hone the fine art of reaching out to people (the scientific term is "sliding into DMs"). When I couldn't find this one interesting person who I wanted to talk to on social media, I sent her an email. The subject line conveyed how absurd it was to start a friendship over email: "I am hereby submitting my application for your friendship."

She responded with eleven paragraphs, which made me like her enough to meet her on FaceTime at 5:55 a.m. the next day (time zones are a beast). We talked for three hours about everything and nothing at all.

Out with shallow talk, in with deep questions. People reciprocated. I realized that we were all just little amoebas bumbling around. If we did away with the notion of having to appear fine, and shared little bits of ourselves with each blue-and-white text bubble, the heart on the other side of the screen would be there to catch us. We'd walk away a little warmer and fuzzier than we were before.

I recognized that other people are lonely—just like me. Text friendships allow us to be vulnerable. Once we were willing to make the leap, we quickly reached the depth of friendship non-pandemic friendships take years to build to, talking about the worries and stressors and the loneliness we feel. We know these vulnerable pieces of others without even knowing what their voices sound like or how their eyes crinkle when they laugh. Send me a voice memo? I ask. How tall are you? I want to be able to make sure my conception of you is the right height. What's your favorite color?

I've heard that, paradoxically, in-person friendships are actually moving more slowly than text friendships are; perhaps, in-person friendships follow the usual small-talk dance.

2020 poured grief, anxiety, fear, and injustice into the soup of uncertainty of growing up. Although the world that we knew may have fallen apart, life, laughing, and love continues. Those pockets of color and warmth break up a lonely fog.

"Social Distance Summer" by Haven Hutchison, 17, Layton, Utah

Teenagers wanted to have the best summer ever, and it was canceled in March.

A few days before this picture was taken, my friend texted me wanting to hang out but also be six feet apart.

My friends and I all decided on a day to drive to a parking lot. We just sat in a circle and talked for about four hours. It was one of the best nights of my quarantine.

All summer, my Instagram feed was filled with people throwing their own proms and finding fun ways to make this summer the best despite the pandemic. Finding a way to be happy in hard times is essential to making it through.

"Friendship" by Phoebe He, 15, New York City ▲

This painting is a tribute to the fact that even though we can't physically see each other, my friends and I still support and love each other in any way possible.

They have been there when my grandmother passed and there to celebrate even the smallest victories, like the time we all stayed up till 3 a.m. to see if I got into a club I tried really hard to apply to.

My friends have made this unusual time bearable.

"Friendship" by Kavya Shah, 14, Secaucus, New Jersey

This is a recreation of a photograph that my friends and I took the first time we met during this pandemic. Before this, I took them for granted and we all would be on our phones most of the time we were together.

We didn't meet up in-person for a very long time for each other's safety but we knew we had to for eighth grade graduation. I had always imagined walking down the auditorium wearing a cap and gown and being handed my diploma. Never would I have ever thought that I would be graduating through a video. We decided to have a socially-distanced picnic celebration. Sitting in the green grass and fresh air, we reminisced about "the good times." ▼

"Two Friends in a Breakout Room: An Excerpt from a Spoken-Word Poem"
by Opal Jane Ratchye, 16, San Francisco

u look different

i guess we haven't seen each other in awhile

yeah, i've melted, smelted, ready to be poured into a new mold, just when I thought i'd found

myself again

oof, i hate when that happens

ya, totally

i've really missed seeing you around

i've missed all the little mundane conversations we've had

i've missed all the little things

in the end those little things are the things i love best

getting a seat on the morning bus ride, and staring out the window into the dull world

and all the mid-class conversations we've had over text when you were three classrooms down

the hall

remember freshman year? we laughed so hard

i don't even remember why, but that doesn't matter

remember walking over the intensely green grass, freshly beheaded with a riding mower

hey?

do you remember like i remember?

hey?

uhhh, I think ur muted

oh yeah, haha, got it now

what were you saying?

"Our Universe" by Jacqueline Ramos and Oyuky Hernandez, 17, Reseda, California

TikTok has been by far the most addicting platform on social media and many from this generation have used this app to express themselves.

We made a TikTok depicting our daily routine as teenagers, illustrating pictures of what could have happened if Covid-19 was never around and what actually happened throughout the whole year.

To start off, we each filmed ourselves in 7 different outfits to represent the 7 days of the week. Our daily routines are now a repetition of doing the same thing over and over again.

See the video at https://www.youtube.com/watch?v=YJuuNq4slww

"A Study Derived from Isolation Summer" by Evin Roen, 16, Tacoma, Washington

In the "before times," I didn't spend nearly this amount of time on my console, and the little time I did spend was on single player games.

This is an accurate representation of the minutes I have played, in total, my top multiplayer (the top four) and single-player (the bottom four) games. It's pretty clear that the majority of Isolation Summer was spent on these games that I can play with friends.

There were a few times where I thought, "Man, I kind of want to play SUPERHOT right now . . ." but mostly I really didn't want to be alone. That's the big thing. These games brought all of my friends together. In fact, it brought me infinitely closer to my old friends in Everett. I had stopped playing with them altogether when I moved because I couldn't really see them anymore. I had made new friends to talk to . . . but now, in the digital age, I realize that's incredibly stupid. Online, it doesn't matter if you're a million miles away or in the same room. ▼

Minutes Spent in Different Games

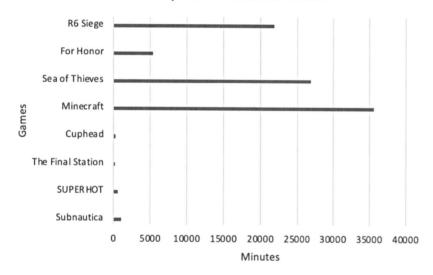

"Highlight" by Brooke Charon, 17, South Milwaukee, Wisconsin ▲

This handwritten note, gifted by a friend delivering cookies, was given to me in April of 2020 after we had officially been sent home from school for the rest of the year. It has been sitting stuck to my window since I received it—just to remember that day.

The feelings that accompany this note describe what it's like to be a teenager in 2020. The dread of being isolated, the loneliness, the ache to be able to see your friends and peers. This note was the highlight of my April.

QUARANTINING WITH FAMILY

*"Usually I would not be caught dead
with three little girls; no teenage boy would."*

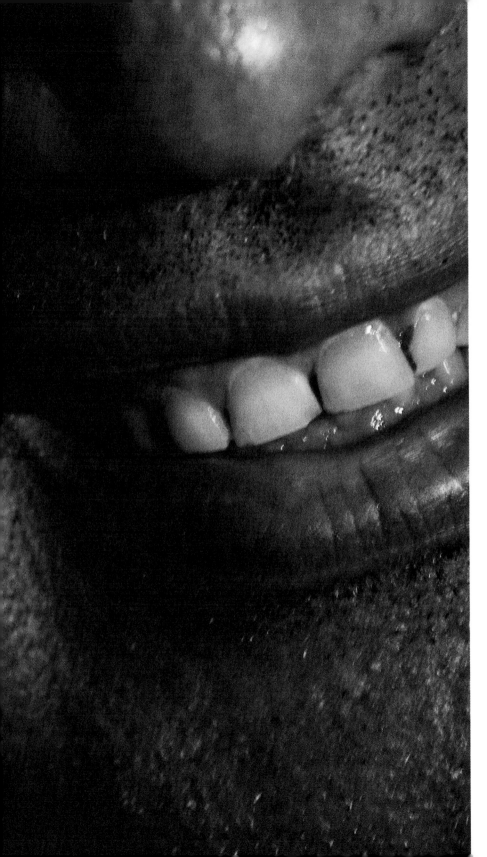

Who knows what my family dynamic will be in the next few years, but I know that I'll miss what I have right now.

My sister is a senior, and I have no idea how I will survive when she goes to college next year. During quarantine, we would drive around our neighborhood blasting Kesha and screaming the lyrics horribly off key. My dad is taking a new position in his job, and my mom is returning to teaching. Neither of these things were able to happen before we were put on lockdown.

This picture was taken on a rainy day, when I felt inspired to take serious portraits of my family members, to match the mood outside and in the world. Despite my best efforts, nobody took me seriously, and I ended up with a series featuring my mom and dad goofing around and tickling each other.

"Sped Up Time" by Samara Vassell, 16, Brooklyn

From the corner of my eye, I see my sister glare at her Chromebook. Her cheeks puff out, like a blob fish. I wouldn't tell her that, because that'd earn me a slap to the arm, and her slaps hurt. She has the mind of a 12-year-old, but the strength of someone in their mid-twenties.

I reach out a hand, about to pat her on the back. But I don't. I almost ask "What's wrong? How can I help?" But I don't. I've done enough of that over these past months. She doesn't need another person to fuss over her.

Not with mom already hounding her over schoolwork, and screen time, and Covid. With dad on her back about her behavior, and her attitude, and again Covid. With our grandparents worried over her, and her aunts worried over her, and her uncles worried over her. Not when I'm meant to be the only one who isn't overprotective of her.

Not when I'm usually the reason she's annoyed. When I'm the one who pokes, prods, and teases until I get a whack to the arm. When I always laugh with her, or laugh at her, or make her laugh. When I ignore everything wrong going on around us, in order to give her momentary happiness.

I never felt protective of her before. I always saw her as a little sister, usually an annoying one. A little sister who used to tag along, but now keeps to herself. A little sister I'd never openly show affection towards, and who'd rather die than show affection towards me. Someone who, if Covid didn't happen, I wouldn't spend time with. Time I planned to make up when I was older, and my patience didn't run out as quick. When I'm more mature and understanding.

Time that I feel Covid sped up. A process of maturity and responsibility and outright worry, that Covid brought crashing down onto my shoulders. I thought it would take years for me to feel this way towards my little sister. The one who's more like a friend than someone I feel the need to protect. Someone I want to shield from the evils of the world.

She looks at me, eyes wide and lips in a pout. Eyes wide with innocence, hope, and things that have left my own. And I can't stop a smile from curling up on my lips, "You need help with anything?"

She nods, pushes the Chromebook to my lap without a word, leaning onto my shoulder. And the feeling of irritation, that used to make me push her off, isn't really there anymore. It's morphed into warmth, and lets me pull her closer.

"Wait, Did I Just Join My Sister's Friend Group?" by Schuyler Schmitt, 17, Marblehead, Massachusetts

Record scratch *Freeze Frame* You're probably wondering how I ended up in this situation.

Considering I am a 17-year-old boy hanging out with four 7th-grade girls, I have some explaining to do.

My sister, the day before, had got this great idea to walk 15 miles in a day but she could not go alone. It being the middle of quarantine, bored out of our minds, I had nothing better to do. I had started walking some days to relax and kill time. Walking, the most mom-activity ever, was entertaining a teenage boy.

So here I am midday, leaving my house to walk with my sister. I had no idea of where we were going to go. All of a sudden she decided she wants to walk to her friend's house, not a short walk. We walk to the next town over. Yes, the next town. We reach her house and we sit outside talking with the friend. The two of them then decide they want to walk to the other friend's house, it's just down the road. So now there is this teenage boy wandering the streets with seventh graders.

It gets worse. We picked up a third girl from her house. There is me and my sister with her two friends. Usually I would not be caught dead with three little girls; no teenage boy would.

There was one more stop still to come. We went to a third girl's house and this stop is where the picture takes place. The five of us sitting in a circle, the classic six feet of separation being enforced.

It just describes 2020 so perfectly. The fact that there is nothing to do so that I would be in a circle with my sister's friends, not even in a house. All the twists and turns of 2020, just like this walk: supposed to go in one direction but shifting dramatically.

"My Record" by Cici Cao, 16, Great Neck, New York

My family used to be very active, and we would solve most of our problems by going out in person. However, because of the pandemic, we have to rely on phone numbers and websites.

I am the only person in my family who can fluently speak both English and Chinese, so as the translator, I had to make this log. I have been a shy person and a big dial-hater; despite that, I still ended up calling countless times. Everything is a lot and extremely difficult to keep track of.

Even tonight, I had to call 911 for my family and come home late because our car was hit and we couldn't do anything. As I am writing this now, I still have a stupid ton of homework to do. *Sigh*.

```
Parent's and Family Stuff Section:
*Mom and Dad's Unemployment Insurance Benefits:
-Claim Weekly
https://my.ny.gov/LoginV4/login.xhtml
Number: 888-581-5812

Dad's DMV and TLC License:
Apply for Renewal
https://www1.nyc.gov/lars/

Doctor's Appointment Number:
████████████
-Call early to make appointment

Inquire about Unemployment Aid for White Card:
888-328-6399

Inquire about Mom's Insurance
800-732-8939
And the Car's Insurance Number
800-364-7045

The number for Bank of America:
-the case on 10/23
800-432-1000

Personal Section:
Mental Health Hotline: 516-679-1111
```

"Reunited" by Olivia Nevin, 14, Grapevine, Texas

Reunited. After two weeks of total isolation, my father could finally reach out and hug us. Until that point, he had remained confined within the walls of his own bedroom. When he was too weak to get up, we secured our masks to check in on him or deliver meals. We kept our distance, praying no one else would catch the virus.

But in this moment, shortly after we received my father's negative results for Covid-19, our family felt whole again. The embrace between my father and eldest sister made up for all the empty "air-hugs" we had been forced to endure.

I sit and listen to the ambience of my family room.

My family fights over our hundredth game of Clue;

Yelling if it was the candlestick or the wrench,

Or who looked at whose paper.

The television blares the same ads over and over

Staged Zoom calls,

Annoyingly fake families laughing and singing kumbaya.

I let the noise of my family muffle,

And the TV sounds melt into a soft hum in the background.

My eyes fix dazedly on the screen;

the light burning my eyes.

I swear I've seen the same lady five times.

Her face plastered with a smile saying everything will be okay.

I roll my eyes.

One more toilet paper joke and I might lose my last shred of sanity.

"One Busy Household" by Atallah Allen, 16, Richmond, California

Before the pandemic, I would always take my dogs to the dog park without worrying about someone being six feet away from me. Now the dogs are limited to just the backyard. We make it work by playing fetch and tug-of-war.

In this photo my dog Tony is barking at my cousin because he wants to play with the basketball. But my cousin keeps ignoring his vocal outbursts. The dog behind me, Molly, is going crazy trying to tear up her bed for no reason. The dogs are restless because they don't like being cooped up in a limited space every day. They're not used to it and don't want to get used to it.

I'm simply laughing into my cousin's shoulder because he'd made a funny comment while I was trying to get everyone to pose for the picture for the 10th time.

When my sister Claire turned 18, I gave her a photo album of pictures of her, me and the rest of my family. They were annotated with notes like "Ridin' in style" beside kindergarten Claire riding a bike in a floppy, colorful winter hat too big for her head.

She was so old to me—18, an adult, a high school graduate entering a world away from home. I was a middle schooler who couldn't imagine myself fitting into a world outside of my family. I was afraid she would forget me. So I gave Claire the photo album to bring a bit of myself into that world with her.

Years later, in 2020, on the precipice of my 18th birthday, I was still at home, and she was back there with me. The photo album was there too, meaning we really were stuck.

While I lost my senior spring, my sister was a 23-year-old stuck at home, and unsure when she had to drive across the country to start a future that has not permitted her to return home for months because of the risk of infecting our family.

Quarantine has taken away so much.

But it also brought us a reminder of what comes with sisterhood.

In April, when I logged off my final high school class, we went for a walk. We ended at an overlook enveloped in green.

"It would be nicer if this wasn't all sewage," she said.

I laughed.

She would talk more than I did. Sometimes she told me the same story twice—days or weeks apart—but I let her keep talking.

Years before, she taught me to love nature. On our walks, she taught me how to use nature to cope.

And, at home, we taught each other to keep hope. She threw mini rubber dinosaurs at me to make me smile on my last day of classes. I made her a sign for her birthday and hung it in the kitchen as a surprise. We sat together water coloring. We walked side by side.

But, in a matter of weeks, she learned she could move out, she packed and she left.

Her car had clothing and memories stuffed into a carrier on the roof and every corner of the seats and trunk. Jeans. A raincoat. The green-blue shirt I wanted when we went thrift shopping, but finders-keepers. Hand sanitizer. Paper towels. Sheets. The gas pedal I mistook for the brake pedal the one time I'd driven her anywhere. Sneakers. Sandals.

No photo album.

The photo album is at home, stuck with me. A bridge between lives, between the continental United States, between sisters.

"Present Haze" by Gabrielle Beck, 16, Tenafly, New Jersey

I entered my grandparent's apartment in Howard Beach, Queens to find the same smell of fish from the bay permeating the walls and the same sly smile greeting me at the door. Everything felt the same, but everything was different.

I was no longer a carefree child running through the halls. I was now a teenager aware of the world's most pressing issues. I wanted to escape my bleak reality; I wanted to live without the constant friction of latex gloves between my hands; I wanted to forget the sound of Purell landing on my fingertips.

While I couldn't come to terms with the present, my grandpa accepted his isolated and confined reality. He perpetually spent his days in his chair viewing the news and the slow drift of smoke coating the walls. Every weekend I would visit him and watch the haze of smoke linger in the air.

"Nougat Candy" by Yishu (Aimee) Yu, 16, Wellesley, Massachusetts

February: Major shutdown of over 48 cities in China.

The bell rang.

"Merci les filles!" My French teacher ended her class as always. Calling me aside, she reached into a metal box and placed a small cube in my hands, "This is only for my Chinese students." She winked at me. I stared at my palm—nougat candy with almonds—my favorite.

Pray for your family.

June: Death toll passed 100,000 in the US.

Mother and I have been quarantining with my jiujiu (uncle) and jiuma (aunt), in their house in North Carolina. I'd just FaceTimed with my grandma, who was still reeling from a break up with her college friend over a petty political difference. Of course, now it seems to go without saying, we cannot be friends with even one disagreement. Grandma told me the news in China: the exact location of each infected person was released to the public in order to keep track of positive cases, down to which car of the subway they were on. The deeper I thought, the scarier it became knowing that my grandma's phone had been with her all day.

A policy, made for the sake of security, was creating paranoia among the people it was trying to protect; a social dilemma, with no absolute right or wrong, was forcing us to isolate and have polarized opinions. So it was with my family, and everyone else.

I heard the adults talking downstairs. My uncle's words like "essential" and "protection" compelled themselves above my mother's "privacy" and "rights" while I wondered whether their argument was even necessary at all. Uncle's voice sounded like a stranger to me, more pompous than patient, more combative than comforting.

In my memory, he was tall enough for me to swing on his arm, and had smile lines clearly visible on his face. I remembered the temperature of his hands over mine when he held my fishing rod with a spotted bass hanging by the hook, and sunshine bouncing up and down on the surface of the Atlantic Ocean.

Hold on to your loved ones.

October: Last month of quarantine before I return home.

Mother asked me a question after we booked our flight back to Beijing: "Which is more valuable, security or freedom?" I did not think anyone was sure, yet they all acted like they did.

When I was packing, I searched for the nougat candy in my bag. Families and friends could sometimes fall into conflict when the world was already in chaos, but a piece of candy offered by a kind-hearted soul, a special sweetness lingering in my mouth, would be enough to hold me together.

Find your way back home.

NAVIGATING ROMANTIC RELATIONSHIPS

"If I send you a meme, will you fall in love with me?"

"a collection of texts you sent me at ten o'clock on a wednesday night"
by Maggie Munday Odom, 17, High Point, North Carolina

If I send you a meme,
will you fall in love with me?

    Will you gaze into your
    phone's blue light
    like it is my eyes?
    Will your fingers flutter
    across your screen
    like it is my body?
    Will you cling to your last
    five percent battery
    like it is my embrace?
    Will you kiss every pixel of me
    like the internet doesn't exist
    and it is only us?

Let's buy an apartment
with windows for walls,
turn off all the lights and look out
at the city,
watching the Wi-Fi
bounce off the buildings,
gazing out at the web of souls
tied together by satellite signals.

    The only you that is here
    is a grey bubble whispering a risky "I love you"
yet my heart still quivers with all this awakening.

"Digital Silence" by Christina Wang, 18, Alpharetta, Georgia

On a day there shouldn't have been any flights, white ramrod strikes of jet stream ran like cat scratch across the blue meat of the sky. I was sitting up at my desk in this unforecasted summer, not an inch of the lovely romanticism I was meant to promise.

There I stayed from March to May, eight hours a day, burning my fingers on my overheating computer as I pressed them into W-A-S-D, playing lagged-out Blitz in Minecraft. Bored the minute I started playing, I was doing it because you asked. It was the only way we were spending time together, even if you didn't talk. I would "get on," as it consistently appeared in my messages, and then become privy to digital silence unless someone killed you.

Sometimes you would speak. To me. You would beg me late into the night to keep playing.

"Please don't leave."

"What difference would it make?" I said, staring longingly at my bed. "We don't talk. It's the same as if you were alone."

"Because I don't want to be alone."

Sometimes you would tell me about your life on the other side of the country.

"School was canceled for the rest of the year."

"Out with not a bang but a whimper."

"Sounds like a bang to me. An unprecedented fucking bang."

Mostly, if you did speak, it was about the game.

"Which level ten kit should I get?"

"I don't care."

So much was carried in our quiet, I wonder if you could feel it. I wasn't trying to get you to love me again, as you had before you asked out your girlfriend, at least not actively. I had stared into the maw of not being loved and learned to swallow it. If not that, I could just hold it in my throat. I accepted, like a ship crashing into my rib cage, instead of the "goodbye, love you" of old times, the line could just cut out.

Loading up a game I learned to hate and killing the time that was supposed to be so ample and precious, I was here because, like you, I didn't want to be alone. It would run in the back of my mind like a second tab but I could ignore it when I was with you. No one else was occupying eight hours of my day.

Towards the end, I realized though, unlike how it was for you, the silence meant being with you was the same as being without you. I was alone even though you were right there.

"Pandemic Boyfriend: A Song" by Amelia Ross, 15, Providence, Rhode Island

This pandemic gave me a quarantine boyfriend

He's pretty great

We FaceTime nearly every minute of
every single day

It gets kinda boring, but we're both bored
so no one's really at fault

I wish this was nearly over, but I'm
afraid it's not

This pandemic boyfriend

Yeah he's pretty cool

He makes me wanna do things

But I have online school

This pandemic boyfriend

Is something new

Sitting here without him

Makes me wonder if it's true

When you talk every day

There's nothing left to say

Oh by the way

I went for a two mile walk outside

This pandemic boyfriend

Is getting less cool

Don't really wanna do things

Cuz I have online school

This pandemic boyfriend

Isn't something new

Sitting here without him

Makes me wonder if it's true

Staying up all night

Isn't fun

When he won't wake up

'til one

Here I am, wide awake

You are my mistake

Here I am, wide awake

Hope I don't make your heart break

That pandemic boyfriend

Wasn't pretty cool

We never did things

When there was no school

That pandemic boyfriend

Is old news

Sitting here alone

Not thinking of you

See the video at https://www.youtube.com/watch?v=9IDV5TeHBOA

During my relationship w/ ~~[redacted]~~ there was always this underlying current of ANXIETY in concern w/ my relationship w/ her. I was so worried that I was too young & she would realize how silly & stupid I am & be embarrassed or regret being w/ me. I was so so worried abt what other ppl would think of us, whether they would understand how serious we are, ~~or that~~ or believe us when we say we are in love. (man I still do. ~~But my anxiety—~~) You could get all my anxiety but it was constant. I need to [...] that, & its crazy its taken me so [...] man its insecurity/ internalized homophobia [...] been from my mom) Like whenever she wasn't [talking] to me I assumed she was angry at me → coz my mom acts that way. Or if she wasn't [constantly] happy & talking to me, she didn't like me anymore & [...] we were [...] awkward. Bruh am I just dealing w/ social anxiety/ regular anxiety.

"Conocer vs. Saber" by Gabrielle Fischberg, 17, New York City

I had gotten broken up over FaceTime from my first serious relationship and was still really torn up about it. In the diary entry, I wrote about the immense anxiety I experienced over the course of my relationship that stemmed from a deep fear of not being enough for my ex, and the excruciating shame of admitting that I loved another woman.

I think my tendency to draw and paint self-portraits is indicative of the self-examination I was doing over quarantine. With the loss of an important relationship, I was trying to put together a cohesive idea of who I was in the absence of someone I loved. I had spent so long defining myself in terms of another person, and now I had to figure that out on my own.

"FaceTime?" by Erin Chase, 17, Buchanan, Michigan

Lots of people go on first dates every day. They are beyond awkward. People don't know each other and they are trying so hard not to say the wrong thing.

"Is my hair okay?"

"Should I have put on more makeup?"

Now, imagine being a teenager. There are extra pressures.

"I can't embarrass myself or I will never live it down."

"Will he think I'm pretty?"

This was my first quarantine date.

I sat on my bed stressed out of my mind, worrying about first-date problems.

BzzzZZzzz.

BzzzZZzzz.

My phone began to ring and the knots in my stomach began doing somersaults.

Why was I so nervous? We had known each other for years.

. . . Maybe that's why.

There was more on the line than just embarrassing myself. If I messed up this relationship, I would be losing a really good friend.

"Hello?"

It was more of a question than a statement. I smiled the most awkward smile in the world.

"Hi."

The voice was timid. The freckle faced kid, my boyfriend, smiled, believe it or not, an even more awkward smile.

. . . .

. . . .

. . . .

. . . .

The silence was maddening.

"How—"

"Wha—"

Great, now we were both speaking over each other.

"You can go," he said.

"Oh, no, you can go," I said.

"You look . . . nice," he said.

There was hesitation. Now I was more nervous.

The conversation went on like this. Awkward speaking, awkward pause, awkward speaking, awkward pause. It was a relief to get off of the call, but I couldn't wait for the next one.

FaceTime dates became a regular Friday night thing after that.

SURVIVING SCHOOL

"I start my sophomore year sitting cross-legged on my bed waiting to 'enter' my Physics class."

"Letter to My Teacher" by Andrew Badhwa, 16, Saint Louis Park, Minnesota

Dear Ms. A.,

I hate school. I always have for as long as I've walked the earth. I hate getting up so early even when the sun is sleeping. I hate the hours of endless lessons and the mountain of homework that I carry home. I hate how there are packed hallways and constant noise. I hate thinking of what others think of me. I hate having to be in groups with people I barely know.

But you know what, Ms. A.? I miss school. I miss the interactions I had with people who were just acquaintances. I miss the teachers I got every year who would always be different and unique in their own way. I miss the loud and chaotic place that was a school. I miss the thought of wondering what others are thinking about me.

People for as long as I remember would be so worried about the way they dressed and looked, or wish they could take back some stupid thing they said. I'm not saying these things shouldn't be worried about, because we all have these issues or have done something we wish we could take back. But you know what's worse than worrying about what others think of you? The thought that no one is thinking of you at all. This is the scariest thing I learned from Covid-19.

Showing up to a dead silent class with virtual people, just a teacher talking to a bunch of black boxes. Would anyone in the world really miss one black box? Who would notice? The attendance sheet? School isn't perfect, but you can still find enjoyment in it. Waking up every morning to go to a class with no one has zero enjoyment. I am struggling so much with school now. Some people can thrive with little help and time, but I am not one of those people. I need extra instructions and a real person I can talk to. I know this is a problem so many other kids are facing just like me, and I deeply hope that we will all be back in the classroom, in person, again soon.

Sincerely,
Andrew Badhwa

"Long Gone" by Brandon Yeo, 15, Issaquah, Washington

This painting is a snapshot of my memory of the last day before quarantine started. I am standing in the middle of nowhere, as a school bus disappears into the horizon.

I made this painting to symbolize what every teenager is experiencing collectively in this time. This year has left us hopeful of the day the school bus will return to us again. ▶

"A Student's Guide to Surviving Zoom University" by Kelsey Smith, 19, San Antonio, Texas

1. Never willingly choose an 8 a.m. In person or not. You're still not going to get out of bed.

2. You can hop on a minute before class starts. Or the minute it starts.

3. Your professor will freeze up . . . and probably say the most important thing about the assignment that's due tomorrow. But don't worry. You'll figure it out (hopefully).

4. There is a gallery button view to see all of your classmates, but don't worry about recognizing them, you won't know what they look like since their camera isn't on. But you'll know all their names!

5. Virtual clubs are *all* the rage. Join one, but a warning, there will be an awkward silence.

6. Key to surviving in small breakout rooms: small talk. Or just turn your camera off and say nothing.

7. Key to surviving in large breakout room. See advice for #6.

8. Choose the best background that represents your personality, especially if you do not want the whole university to see your messy childhood bedroom. I've seen that pink butterfly wallpaper. Everyone knows what I'm talking about.

9. You can leave whenever you want and no one will notice. There's no door. It's nice to get a head start on that grilled cheese for lunch.

10. When your teacher doesn't teach and Professor Google can't teach you. Q drop.

11. And last of all, take a break. Watch some TV. Look out a window. Go outside for the first time this week. You need a moment of serenity in all of this chaos, and since classes are online in the spring too.

"Algebra Class" by Camila Salinas, 15, Frisco, Texas

I wake up, go to school, and sit at my desk. I do some work, the bells rings, go to the next class. I do some work, the bells rings, go to the next class. I get home, sit down, do my homework and catch up on a show. I go to sleep and I repeat. The pandemic has affected our lives in many significant ways, but for me it has just been isolating.

Although my algebra classroom can range from five to 30 students, it feels as though there is only you. And for students learning from home, the situation is worse. They are literally by themselves.

"On or Off?" by Astrid Utting, 15, San Francisco

I start my sophomore year sitting cross-legged on my bed, waiting to "enter" my Physics class. I smooth the wrinkles in my blouse and tuck a stray hair behind my ears, ready to stare at a video of myself all day. Instead of my usual carefully planned school outfits, I'm rocking a pair of old sweatpants and fuzzy pink socks. I select "video on" and hold my breath as the screen loads, anxious to meet my new classmates. Instead, I'm greeted by a sea of black screens, some with names, others accompanied by profile photos of cartoon animals and flowers. I quickly turn my video off too.

Wouldn't it be better socially and academically if we could see each other? Possibly, but I understand that it's an equity issue. At a public high school like mine, students are not required to turn their videos on because not everyone has a home that they feel comfortable sharing with their classmates.

In fact, I've been angling my camera so that my background is my bedroom wall because I feel uncomfortable showing people I barely know the room that I share with my little sister. Her unmade bed and stuffies litter the floor, my scattered polaroids washi-taped to the wall.

Frankly, the option to have your video off is one of the few perks of distance learning. Hair rumpled, you could be munching on tortilla chips in bed while the teacher lectures, and no one would know . . .

But when everyone has their videos off, we can't share a knowing smile when our eccentric substitute says something weird. When the teacher asks a question and the class remains silent, she can't see that I'm listening, I just don't know the correct answer. When class ends and I unmute to say goodbye, I wonder if my teacher even knows who's talking to them.

It doesn't look like we're returning anytime soon. Not to schools like mine, with no way to safely socially distance in a building built for half the current student population. In a time when we've already lost so much social contact, do we really want to go through a whole school year knowing our classmates only by the names on their screens?

Lately, I've made an effort to turn my video on in every class. Last week, when I was the only one to show my face, I felt weird and awkward. Did anyone even care, or were they all staring at me? But finally, one girl turned her video on too! Huh, she had a short brown bob, I'd pictured her as a blonde! A look of relief passed over her face, and then she smiled at me.

Forget to mute

Take a break to vent   "Please mute"

Stare at screen apathetically   "Cameras on please!"

Cry out   "No recorded lectures…"

Punch an object   Internet crash

Reset wifi router   Email teacher

Binge Netflix, whenever   Teacher ignores

"Bond" with family   "Tuition discount? Um…"

"Sorry, my dog is loud…"   Ignore class

"REAL world applications!"   "…here's a group project…"

Meditation doesn't really apply to me   "…no, you can't choose who…"

Joining class   Eat (again)

"Hello, guys?   "Sorry, no scholarships….Check in a few years?"

Test canceled?   I'm just FINE

"…10 page research paper…"   Orders takeout

"…Single-spaced…"   "Yes, I'm eating healthy, MOM!"

Cry   Check more emails

"Call technical support…"   Email teacher

"Time to stretch!"   …Nope, nothing yet.

"…fresh air…"   Lectures posted, I think!

"Among Us!"   "Wait, there's smog outside?"

Yoga, not

"LUNCH"

ZOOM LUNCH WAS DIFFERENT.
ZOOM LUNCH WAS WEIRD.
I WAS USED TO HANGING OUT WITH MY
FRIENDS AND CATCHING UP ON ALL THE
NEWS OVER LUNCH.
IT SEEMED A LITTLE DISJOINTED
HANGING OUT OVER ZOOM.
AWKWARD.

"Zoom" by James Tyler, 13, Isle of Palms, South Carolina

I compiled this piece while isolated at my house after school abruptly closed without warning on March 13, 2020. My only contact with my former school life was via Zoom.

Hey! It's me, your backpack!

Don't recognize me? It's probably because I lost some weight over quarantine. The crumbled homework, stuffed notes, and chubby folders now sleep in your desk drawers instead of my clothed stomach. Don't get me wrong, I love my thin limbs and sprouting abs—never mind that was just a layer of dust—but what's the point when I'm stuck in the dark abyss of your closet, where no one can see my glow-up? And your third-grade camp shirts don't count.

But do you really not remember anything? I was your loyal study buddy from day one, protecting your precious cargo even when the sky wept, concealing your test scores especially when they were bad, and babysitting your homework on days they didn't get enough love from you. I never said a word every time you dropped me onto the cold, hard school floor, not even when your gaunt thermos leaked your smelly fish soup through my nylon walls. I always had your back—and the fact that you had to go to physical therapy three times a week because of shoulder pain is not my fault. Okay, so now you remember me?

Well, what are you waiting for? Come rescue me from your dump of cartoon camp shirts. Sling me onto your shoulders like you did until school moved into your house. And most importantly, tell me how skinny I look.

Why thank you, you really didn't h—hello? You still there? Because I'm still here: in the cavernous darkness of your closet, alone. I would love to be taken to my first-class seat, any day now. Well fine, I suppose economy seating by your bookshelf could suffice. You still there? Just so you know, anywhere outside of your damp closet works, too.

Even though you no longer need me to carry chipped pencils and bloated folders, I'm versatile! Hanging out with friends? I can carry extra masks, gloves, hand sanitizer, and a six foot measuring tape. Going for a hike? I can hold your water bottles, ice packs, Canon DSLR, mini cooler, electric fan—or I could just pay for your physical therapy fee instead.

The bottom line is that I do something. I would give up my baby abs from five months of Chloe Ting workouts to lend you a hand. I wouldn't mind sleeping next to the cardboard-esque camp shirts just to do you a favor. All the same, let me help—preferably with pencils, folders, and notebooks—but I'm okay with anything, just as long as I'm with you.

Love, Your Backpack

"Covid Garage Classroom Tour" by Christine Chang, 13, San Carlos, California

Michael, our mailman, and my stuffed lion made up my entire social circle.

The spring of 2020, I woke up each morning with a pit in my stomach. Same eggs and toast every day, three hours of schoolwork, and the rest of the day wasted, staring at the ceiling and eating a questionable amount of Doritos. I think my fingers are still stained orange. As May came and went, I wondered when I would ever return to school.

When my middle school announced we would be virtual again this school year, I looked my stuffed lion in the eye and told him we were having none of it. I ran downstairs to assess our garage. It wasn't much, but I had a grand plan. I spent dinner convincing my parents to move their cars out. I gave it a fresh coat of paint, added free furniture from Craigslist, and dollar-store decorations.

With the California wildfires, the first days of school were smoky, and my plan couldn't come to fruition. However, the smoke cleared, and four of my friends biked up the hill to my house, grinning awkwardly.

Instead of staring at little faces on Zoom alone all day, we now laugh during lunch, choreograph and perform dances during breaks, and spend school days working on homework together. We've all pitched in to furnish our space with tables, couches, and even a bean bag. We've drawn posters to hang on the walls to make the space our own. We pull the strings of our friendship close together. We fondly call what is essentially our clubhouse the Garage Classroom. With masks, social distancing, and both doors open for fresh air, I feel safe.

More than that, I feel connected. I belong.

See the video at https://www.youtube.com/watch?v=Cf8UAOjd3cQ

"Gap Year?" by Nina Chang, 18, Providence, Rhode Island

At the beginning of 2020, I was on an all-time high. I had gotten into the school of my dreams, I had started a small but lucrative business of painting pet portraits for people in town, and had already begun searching for a college roommate.

Well, 2020 had different plans for all of us.

I began to question if going to college this year was really the best choice. This piece is how I've decided to capture this blur of thoughts and images that consumed me as I tried to make the hard decision.

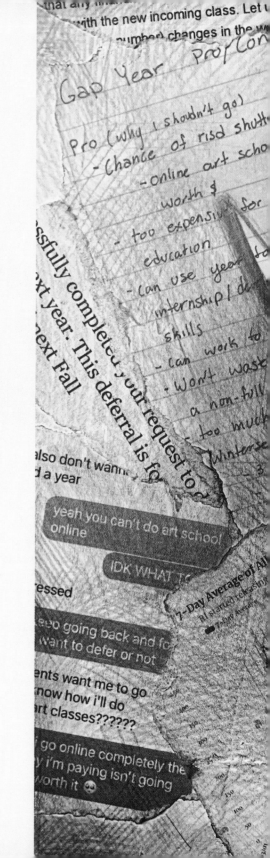

"Freshman Year at Corona High School" by Anisha Menezes, 14, Grapevine, Texas

I have always been what people call an "overachiever." I show up late to color guard practice with my hair wet from my morning swim practice, and despite my sore arms, I spend an hour tossing my weighted metal flag. I finish my AP Computer Science assignments during downtime at swim meets.

But there are only 24 hours in a day, and 7 days in a week, and I was always missing out on something.

Now I find myself with more time I could dedicate to my interests. With everything suddenly online, my next activity was only a few clicks away. ▼

"My 2020 in a Nutshell" by Kelly Guo, 17, New York City ▲

This painting captures my life in recent months. The two uniforms represent one of the biggest changes—sports. I am on a team all year, but the pandemic has stripped that away from me.

The watercolor palette along with a Pratt Institute handbook represents the college application deadlines ahead of me. How am I going to compete with other talented artists when I've barely started my college portfolio?

The Instagram page on my phone shows online activism trending as American youth spread awareness about issues of all kinds. Who knows where this will lead?

WORKING

"We are the most expendable workers
in the country, but also the people
at the frontline of a nationwide battle."

124

"Fruitful Labor for a Border" by Glorybelle Barrios, 15, Miami, Florida

Through the knife-thin screen of my iPhone, the leaden eyes of my father spoke: "Perdí mi trabajo, pusita"—I lost my job, honey.

Now here I stand, frozen, but calculating means in my head to provide an income for my father: paid internship, tutoring more students, coding websites for pay, selling poems. I beg him to not worry—"Papa, I can fix this. I will find you a job." He knows he must wait in the same manner he crossed rivers, bundling clothes on his head to not get it soaked.

This is the novel normalcy of a first-generation teen US citizen. We have never ceased to stand upon a needle to weave various strings into a solution: assisting non-English speaking parents in tedious applications for government benefits, searching jobs for our parents, solitarily navigating the US educational system. The pandemic has merely increased our efforts by tenfold, so we are no longer weaving blankets, but convoluted quilts: translating reliable news to our parents due to non-English disconnects in the media, preparing for a consequential election by researching candidates, and learning directly from our parents of the inequities they face from systematic disparities.

"Working During a Pandemic"
by Penelope Cardenas, 17, Chula Vista, California

I took this picture in early April, a few weeks after I started my first job. I had no idea of what was to come.

My job has given me a unique vantage point. Last summer, a parade of cars protesting rent control circled the place. A stream of Black Lives Matter protesters did the same, with phrases like "ACAB" and "Abolish ICE" spray painted onto their vehicles. One car even went through the drive-thru and gave me a sticker of the iconic fist. At one point traffic consisted mostly of Trump supporters protesting as well, their American flags and banners waving as they drove past.

Working where I do, you get to see and interact with a very diverse range of people. In a politically charged year, with most people identifying very strongly one way or the other, I've been gifted pamphlets, spiels, tiny flags, and stickers by passionate customers ready to share their beliefs.

"Texting Mom During Quarantine" by Jacob, 13, Osprey, Florida

Although I'm not much of a sleep-in kind of person, I was also assigned a lot of chores during that time, and they were not fun.

"Taking Advantage of Time" by Kurt Plakans, 16, Danvers, Massachusetts

I live in a town where it is common to own a boat since we are located on the water. To teach myself how to lobster, I started with hours of research, planned all my steps, got the supplies and a required license. The deeper I got into it, the more I realized how much goes into lobstering. You have to set up all the traps with rope calculations for the depth of low and high tides in the spots where you are going to drop them.

Eventually, I started a small business with two friends. We had to maintain the traps, making sure there was bait and refilling them every three days. We had to catch the bait on our own and make sure we always had enough before going out to check the traps.

The most memorable and rewarding moment was when we caught the lobster in the picture. This lobster was massive—five pounds. It was just under the maximum size and we ended up giving it to my friend's dad for his birthday.

This year is a year I will remember for the rest of my life. This year the entire country shut down but also the year when I learned new things about myself.

Photo by Craig Michalowski

"A Farmer's Quarantine" by Jadon Flinton, 15, Galway, New York

When you hear people's stories of quarantine they talk about how they were stuck at home not able to see close friends and family, but it isn't that way for farmers.

Let's start from the day it all changed. The 14th of March we get the email saying schools aren't going back until after spring break, and the first thing my dad and I start talking about is the bigger projects around the farm that need to get done and what I can start working on.

The next day I am rushing my dad back to the house while calling my mom after he just lost part of his finger doing one of those projects. My mom took him to the ER, but chores still had to get done. They got home around 8 that night after they amputated the smashed part. But since we live on a farm, life had to go on and we still had to do the same dangerous jobs every day.

After it started warming up and the fields were growing and my dad was getting used to the 9 and ¾ finger life, as we call it, I managed to finish a project I started when I was 12. It took me about 3 years but it was a huge milestone: getting to drive this tractor, which has been in the family for 45 years, to my grandparents' farm to get my grandfather's reaction.

In August, my dad had to travel, so second-cut hay was up to me. By September 1st at 15 years old I did about 2,000 bales almost completely on my own. In the end "Corona time," as my friends call it, has helped me grow up some and in a weird way I'm thankful for that. I wouldn't trade it for anything.

"Essential Worker?" by Ava Isabella Kendra Haddock, 16, Carlsbad, California

In June, I joined the official work force as a busser. As adults with health fears leave, students like me fill jobs as everything from lifeguards to child care providers. Poetically, you could argue that student employees valiantly enforce regulations with an often hostile and polarized public, doing the work necessary to keep the community running. You could also say that we selfishly enable a broken system, and put our families at risk. As Covid-19 hot spots emerge in restaurants like mine, they expose the uncomfortable moral gray area of choosing to work.

In comparison to more essential jobs, student jobs seem frivolous. We are the most expendable workers in the country, but also the people at the frontline of a nationwide battle. As I clean up birthday dinners and vaguely illegal live-music nights, I want to quit. Most customers, and even my boss, act with little regard to public safety. Trying to enforce regulations feels like trying to stop a tidal wave of disregard with a bucket.

But the false facade of safety enforced by laughing bartenders and smiling customers is alluring. Fears of financial insecurity also smooth over most remaining health concerns. Besides, if I quit, there will be little impact. I'm easily replaceable.

Every time I work, I choose to roll the dice. When I talk about the summer of 2020, I'll say I marched, and I'll say I worked. I don't know if I'll be proud.

SUPPORTING THE BLACK LIVES MATTER MOVEMENT

*"It has encouraged me and
an entire generation of young
people to speak up."*

"The Right Side of History" by Serynn Nowlin, 17, Buchanan, Michigan

"Hands up! Don't shoot! Hands up! Don't shoot!"

The chant quivers its way from my hoarse vocal cords to join the hundreds of others echoing through the charged air. My arms ache slightly from the weight of my makeshift cardboard sign, held up high for all to see. It reads Silence Is Violence. BOOM. BOOM. BOOM. Ricocheting off of my ribs, my heart chants along with me, both emboldened by the action I'm taking, yet terrified of what it could so easily become.

Beside me marches my best friend, the one who drove me here despite the disapproval of my parents. "Why do you even want to go? It's way too dangerous . . . especially in that town. I don't get why it's such a big deal." Their words surround and suffocate my brain, adding to the intense atmosphere.

Up ahead, a small but mighty cry tears through the cacophony of the crowd and my mind. A voice that is high-pitched and accompanied with slight mispronunciations, unmistakable trademarks of a child. Balancing on the shoulders of one much older, a young girl no more than five years old clings to a bullhorn half her size. Again, the same battle cry erupts from her tiny frame, "No justice, no peace. No racist police."

Inspired by her courage, I shut out the voices in my head and bask in the sheer power of the moment. I am truly humbled by the incredible individuals that surround me—many of us complete strangers—united with the goals of justice and equity. As Breonna Taylor's and George Floyd's names resound through the streets, I find myself realizing the pivotal nature of this moment and that I am on the right side of history.

"Wake Up Alarm" by Jaclyn Maurice, 15, Seattle

When your alarm goes off early in the morning, the last thing anyone wants to do is wake up. The sheets are warm, the air outside is cold, and it's all you can do to stop your heavy head from sinking back into the pillow. It's just that being comfortable is so soothing, and all anyone wants to do is return to dreaming.

It's a similar feeling when, as a white person, we're confronted with the longstanding issues of racism in the United States. I've heard people say that the death of George Floyd is the first wake up alarm, but the hard truth is that Black and Indigenous people of color have been ringing this alarm for decades, calling for systematic reform in every space they enter. Especially as a teen, it feels easier most days to just hit snooze on the problems of our country and go back to sleep.

In a progressive city like Seattle, most of my classmates and peers participate in internet activism. This consists of reposting viral images, spreading resources for involvement, signing petitions, and engaging in online discourse. The issue is that it's very easy to post an image, put down your phone, and feel as though you've fulfilled some kind of duty to activism for the day. Very quickly in the weeks that follow an event such as the death of George Floyd, people just doze off into another desensitized daydream.

Imagine if everyone who professed allyship in the fight against racial injustice refused to return to life as normal. Imagine if everyone made a change no matter how small every day by just donating, or supporting, or protesting. Imagine if every white person dragged ourselves out of bed, and refused to become despondent.

It's an extremely demanding process one goes through when ripping the wool off of one's own eyes. But a bright new sun is rising, bringing with it a new day, and it's past high time everyone woke up.

"He Is America" by Christian Lee, 17, La Habra, California

I stand in solidarity with the Black Lives Matter movement. It has encouraged me and an entire generation of young people to speak up.

I photographed one of my best friends wearing the American flag, because I thought it would be a simple but profound act of protest against racially motivated police brutality.

"Privilege" by Annabella Hong, 15, Silver Spring, Maryland

I am not Black. I do not know what it may be like to be Black. I am privileged and many people in my friend group are also privileged. They have the privilege to simply like a post and move on with their days. They have the privilege to simply add three letters to their bio. They have the privilege to post a black square to their social media and nothing more.

I feel like I've been in a bubble. It's easy to ignore the problem. I don't want to be the person who does nothing with my privilege. I want to educate myself and fight for those whose voices can't be heard on an equal level to mine.

Privilege is the same as power: You have to be responsible for how you use it.

On June 1st, 2020, my brother Nat and his friend were arrested in downtown Philadelphia on suspicion of domestic terrorism. They were at a Black Lives Matter protest following the murder of George Floyd. They were there with masks to protect people from spreading the virus. They also had a baking soda and water mixture which is commonly used to help people who get tear gassed. My brother wasn't at the protest to start violence. He was there to try and help the community.

On that day my brother and his friend weren't the only ones being arrested. There were so many more people taken by the police for doing nothing. He was one of the victims who was wrongly accused and badly treated.

My brother had a dollar bill in his pocket. When he asked for change he wasn't given it so he couldn't make a phone call to our parents. We didn't know where he was for many hours. We didn't know that he was being interrogated by the FBI because the police had accused him and his friend of being domestic terrorists. We didn't know he was in a state prison that had been shut down two years ago because conditions were too bad for prisoners to be there. We didn't know that he spent the night in a jail cell with a Black man who had been so badly beaten by the police he needed Nat to keep him warm all night.

What we did learn after 24 hours of waiting for news and information from the lawyer who was helping our family was that the charges had been dropped. She said that in the years she's been working to help Black and brown men get released from jail not once had she seen a judge drop all charges so quickly. My brother was let free because he is white.

I am a dark-skinned Latino. Ever since my white brother was arrested I started to pay more attention to racial injustice and protests across the country, I have become more aware of my actions. I try to avoid walking around with my hood up. I try to avoid walking around with my hands in my pockets. I try to avoid making eye contact with the police.

Living through all of this has made me worried, not only for myself but for my friends who are also people of color and for others in our community and our country who aren't white. I feel like things need to change although it might take time. I am hopeful that one day the justice system will treat all people fairly no matter the color of their skin.

"Intersectionality" by Edelina Bagaporo, 17, Chula Vista, California

This photo encompasses my own identity as an LGBTQ+ Filipina–American woman. It highlights my role as an ally to the movements of social justice. No longer do I talk about boys or paint my nails, but start to recognize the part I can play in fighting for justice and how to tackle my implicit biases.

Although this was not the summer I was expecting, it truly has brought on tremendous personal growth, which I would not trade for anything.

"Young, Gifted, and Black" by Ella Heldring-Crowther, 17, New York City

This photo was captured during a Black Lives Matter protest on June 19, 2020, in New York City.

Pictured are my friends since 6th grade. On the left is Dana Colyer. She carries a sign that reads "Justice for George Floyd, Breonna Taylor . . ." and countless other names of Black people who have been killed by the police. I think about how many people on Dana's poster deserved to have many more years of curls dancing in the wind.

On the right is Naila Gomez in a black shirt that says "Young, Gifted, and Black." Although her mask covers half of her face, you can see the piercing concern in her eyes.

During the protests, the three of us would often share our frustration with the white adults around us. "They're not chanting at all," we would say or "Why are they talking about the next tattoo they're going to get?" In fact, many times adults would turn around at us and look frustrated that we were yelling so loudly. Why come to a protest if you're not going to protest and yell?

It's clear teenagers won't let the inability to vote stop them from making political change.

"Why Can't I, Why I Can't"
by Christian Isaiah Dorsey-McQueen, 16, Carlsbad, California

Why can't I run—**Ahmaud Arbery**

Why can't I play with a toy gun—**Tamir Rice**

Why can't I wear a hood—**Trayvon Marti**n

Why can't I go to the park with my friends—**Antron, Kevin, Yusef, Raymond,** and **Korey**

I mustn't go on a run or I am a burglar

I mustn't have a toy gun or I am shooting up a place

I mustn't wear a hood or else I am making a lean

I mustn't be with my friends or else I'm a rapist

And here's the reason

I must always bow down to the invisible laws and systems that will always trap me

My stride, my culture, and my *intelligence* will always pose a threat

The way I speak with my deep voice and directness will make people feel
they're being attacked while I am the walking target

Because as a Black male in this society I am forced to be on guard

I have been born a target and every which way I turn I must watch my back

People will always assume the worst about me just because of the color of my skin even though

the worst has been done to me because of the color of my skin.

I fear for my younger brother and sister about how they will be perceived and how their lives can be taken away

I have to say yes ma'am and yes sir so I don't seem threatening and get shot

My world has been set up for me in previous generations before I can do anything

However, here's what I can do

"I [can] no longer accept[] the things I cannot change. I [will] chang[e] the things I cannot accept"—**Angela Davis**

"I can fight by any means necessary"—**Malcolm X**

"I can lead into a better future for the Black community"—**Harriet Tubman**

"I can speak about the problems we face and come up with a solution"—**Frederick Douglass**

"I can educate those who need to be educated so we can all move forward together"—**W. E. B. DuBois**

"Together" by Joyce Weng, 14, New York City

Teenagers took this year to think about what's happening in the world. We teenagers realize the adults we trust are not who they really are. We have to stand up for ourselves and make a change and a lot of this activity happened over social media.

No matter what race, we all came together to create the Black Lives Matter Movement.

Some teenagers who didn't go out there and protest helped from home. We signed all petitions, made donations, and educated ourselves on topics we should have known a long time ago.

"A Wave of Change" by Janie Lee, 15, Marlboro, New Jersey

With somewhat strict parents, I wasn't allowed to go to any of the Black Lives Matter protests or rallies, so I wanted to at least document this momentous time through art.

Covering the eyes, which typically represents someone's identity, the "window to the soul," expresses the idea that prejudices and unconscious racism often keep people from seeing Black people for who they are as individuals.

As a daughter of the Haitian Diaspora, I have seen the beauty of community and the change that can be made when we lovingly uplift each other despite the obstacles stacked against us.

I wanted to display a Black woman freely taking up space and being hyperaware of the camera placed in front of her. Historically, Black folks (particularly Black women) have been tokenized, commodified, and exploited by photographers. Through my work, I wanted to confront that history by centering and focusing on my gaze.

In times of suffering, Black women have cried together, protested together, laughed together, and loved together. Our stories are still being written, and our light will continue to shine once we are gone. "See Me, I See You" is an ode to the power and beauty of Black women.

"My Place" by G. Cole Reynolds, 16, Oakland, California

My 2020 arrived in one of those cardboard boxes that are so ubiquitous on everyone's porches. It was my gift, but my father opened it anyway. Out of the endless abyss of packing peanuts, he procured a Civil War–era cup and a note written in script. Apparently the cup was a possession of some distant relative whom I was named after. This was awesome! It's rare to have a physical link to your family history—especially one that's so hard to navigate.

I'm part Black, but that's hidden behind light eyes and hair caught somewhere between a curl and a wave. I drive without fear of arrest, but it still hurts the same when something racist cuts deep into the core of my identity. So when I read the last line of that note—"he's buried at the Confederate Memorial"—I got the one feeling that all BIPOC know. It's the feeling of moisture from your mouth ending up in your palms—a physical rejection of something so repugnant, it makes you want to puke. It's the feeling of every pair of eyes focusing onto you and being uniquely self-conscious of every heartbeat, every breath. A sickly haze lowered over my vision, and every voice suddenly sounded miles away. That cup is still a link to my history, but how can I live with that history?

I felt confused, hurt, disgusted, but I slowly realized that, actually, I was angry; I felt my family subtly asking: "Which history do you really belong to?" I was trapped, lost in the borderlands between two conflicting parts of society—a pale kid with a Black grandpa on one side, and now, a slaver's legacy on the other.

That same day, 8 minutes and 46 seconds at a Minneapolis street corner broke the collective heart of America. Naturally, I found myself in the sea of people marching for justice, embattled from the emotion of the previous week, but inspired by the revolutionary zeitgeist of the moment.

Growing up in this Manichaean society, there isn't much room for a term like "acceptance" or a concept like "community." But marching alongside people united by their beliefs, it should've been the closest to a community that I could find. Somehow, I felt alone. I felt stranded somewhere between ally and activist—completely invisible to the binary of the United States.

As America tries to understand its racial identity, I commence a similar journey. I'll keep fighting until Black lives matter. And somewhere in the movement, I hope to find the answer to a question that's stuck to me like gum beneath a shoe: Is there a place for me in America?

When the news surfaced of the murder of Ahmaud Arbery, George Floyd, and Breonna Taylor I was distraught and in need of support. My moms are always here for me, but there is something special and necessary about connecting with your peers. I needed a way forward and assumed others felt similarly so I decided to create Mad's Book Club. The club has gone beyond what I imagined. When uncertainty strikes we need connection and community more than ever. Being a teenager is about finding the connection that powers you onward.

"Ashes to Ashes" by Kaltun Mohamed, 17, Minneapolis

First, it was the bank that caught fire. Then the building across the street that helps people find jobs, then the Walgreens. We were standing in front of my neighbor's door when a man came and set several trash cans on fire. I remember my heart jackhammering in my chest as I stood there. My mother yelled at me to grab a hose and my hands shook as we put the fire out together. I didn't sleep that night, after I packed my most important belongings in my school backpack, and neither did the rest of Minneapolis.

The next morning felt like an out-of-body experience. It was all broken glass and smoldering buildings and armed guards with tank guns. I remember feeling a stab in my heart as I swept up the broken glass outside of the corner store that my mother used to walk me to as a child, where they know us by name. There were points, as I watched police officers use tear gas on protesters and walk through the remains of my neighborhood in riot gear to face crowds of civilians, that I felt like my anger would consume me. However, when I went to protests and visited the memorial and heard people speak, I felt the seeds of hope start to grow. I was awestruck to see the amount of people who showed up for clean up efforts, organized food drives and

painted murals. Someone had spray-painted the word "Healing" at the top of what was once a Kmart. As I watched the birds soar past the broken buildings that May afternoon, I realized that resilience is in the very fabric of our community.

In a way, we were always in danger. The fear that I felt that night in May was not a new feeling. It's the feeling I get when I see a police officer come up to a group of my Black classmates at a bus stop, or pull over my mother. My hands shake and my stomach rolls with anxiety. It's the same sickening fear I felt as I watched George Floyd be inhumanely murdered.

In 2021, as the rubble gets cleared and buildings are rebuilt, I hope that we also move forward and rebuild in a way that is conducive to racial justice, together.

WITNESSING ELECTION 2020

"Before this year, I'd never considered myself a political person."

"Now Showing: 2020" by Maddox Chen, 15, Manhattan Beach, California

Using my preferred medium of LEGO bricks, I created a physical mock up of my typical spot of being for the past eight months: glued to a screen, whether that is my phone, laptop, or the TV.

Politics, and more recently, the presidential race, have dominated the airwaves since the onset of the pandemic, and has covered everything, from racial injustice, social inequities, economic disparities to the simple act of wearing a mask.

One cannot refer to the year of 2020 without mentioning the diametric struggle between President Donald Trump and President-elect Joe Biden.

"The 2020 Election Through the Eyes of a Teen" by Madeline Andreatta, 14, Lexington, Kentucky

The past few days were exhausting. I've spent countless hours staring at the TV, watching the votes pour in. I knew the results wouldn't be in on Tuesday night, but I didn't expect it to take until Saturday. When we finally learned the winner, I was so relieved. Biden had won, and that crucial first step was taken. But it was only the first step. There is still so much more to do, and change is only just beginning.

Despite the fact that the election is over, I still find myself appalled at the number of people who voted for Trump again. How could over 70 million people vote for a man who is trying to strip the rights of my brother and my best friend? How could they vote for someone who wants to deport or turn away immigrants like my grandparents? How could they support someone who refused to condemn white supremacy on national television, and whose irresponsible handling of the coronavirus pandemic contributed to nearly 240,000 American deaths? I don't think I will ever understand.

Something that I hear often is, "you're too young to have an opinion on politics." I'm almost 15. I'm old enough to walk into my high school with fears of a school shooting, but I'm not old enough to have an opinion on what we can do to prevent them? I don't understand. I see everything that happens in the world, just like anyone else. I have seen Trump become one of three presidents in US history to be impeached, and not lose any support. When he was elected in 2016, I was five days shy of turning 11. Because I was too young to vote, I thought I was too young to have an opinion. Now, I'm five days shy of 15, and although I am still too young to vote, I've learned that everyone witnesses what happens in our country, and that no one is too young to have an opinion on it.

Before this year, I'd never considered myself a political person. But seeing seemingly ordinary people take charge and fight for racial justice this summer, and watching my cousin continue to fight for better gun control have shown me that anyone can be a political person. I've found a passion for politics that I never imagined I'd have. Although I won't be able to vote for another four years, I will never stop using it to fight for what's right.

"Everlasting Reminder" by Michael Bell, 17, Memphis

When it first appeared, I could hear the moms in their Lululemon track suits talking about property values, hate speech, a great stain on the community, and never being this afraid before.

As I walked to the store, I saw the way people looked at this in horror and then back at me with their eyes never quite adjusting. The store still hasn't taken it down for what reason I don't know, and the longer it stays, the more it digs underneath the nail of my community.

To describe the world as an ugly place would be an understatement. The world is a brutal, heartbreaking, barbaric, grim, chaotic place.

To describe my neighborhood as nice would be an understatement. The schools are good, the streets are clean, the air is clean, the people will smile as they cross the street, the gun boxes are always locked but always ready. The crowning jewel are the many grocery stores with their clean floors, red apples, sushi bars, Starbucks.

I'm only seventeen, I don't know anything, the only thing that I know is that this is a reminder that there is no going back to normal. I wanted to show you something real. The people that have died, the families that are starving, the children that are failing, there is no back to normal for them, so there is no back to normal for us.

"We Couldn't" by Eliza Gilliom, 14, Chapel Hill, North Carolina

In September, as the presidential election neared, I kept finding myself on Zoom calls filled with teens and young adults from all over the country. Some of them were organizers who spoke at protests to hundreds of people, but a lot of them were just kids like me concerned about what the future had in store. We came together on the internet to get voters to the polls. This involved hours of calling, texting, and mailing postcards to voters.

I drew these teens from the safety of my bedroom. Most of the faces in the drawing are strangers I phone-banked with but never spoke to. As teenagers we couldn't vote, but we protested and made thousands of calls.

"Masks Are Political" by Ela Desai, 14, Manhattan Beach, California

The mask. Once, it was only a barrier to respiratory droplets, equipment for personal protection. But in a year with so many exposures—a new virus, deep seated racism, disparities in education, and challenges inherent to democracy—masks have become a statement. This face covering is now a meaningful symbol for the rights of the individual versus the group, the fears of the vulnerable, the comforts of the healthy, and the path to return to a pre-Covid life.

"The Presidential Battle" by Colette Reckamp, 14, Naperville, Illinois

Sung to the tune of "Cabinet Battle #1" from Hamilton

Chris Wallace:
People of America! You could've been doing anything else
 tonight, but you're watching this Presidential Debate.
Are you ready for some serious chaos?
An issue on the table
Public and private healthcare, then why is your plan better
 than your opponents?
Vice President Biden, you have the floor, sir.

Joe Biden:
Obamacare and private insurance
Trump's testing my patience but I've got endurance
Make health care attainable for all kinds of people
We're trying to get everybody here equal
Yeeaahh
But Trump he forgets
He'll abolish health care twenty million people get
His nonexistent plan gives us lots of deaths
And his blabber of fake news is a waste of his breath

Donald Trump:
Fake news!

Biden:
Oh let the press choose; deal with it
We've been struck down by this virus and now we've got to
 heal with it
I won't listen to him, Trump claims
Come on, mature up, do you think this is a game?
In Washington there's decorum to follow, we're polite
Now listen up, 'cause this will be hard to swallow
Trump's health care plan makes him think he's Superman
And it's about time he knows doesn't have a fan
And he's old! That's not a natural color of gold!
Look, we can't let this man go out so uncontrolled!
His own scientists he contradicts
Pick me for a better president forty six

Wallace:
Thank you Vice President Biden.
President Trump, your response?

Trump:
Now Joe, that is all totally fake
What about your sons and all of their mistakes?
Kicked from the army, and please, tell us how
He got all of that money up from Moscow
I'm cuttin' drug prices and two minute slices
Aren't enough to tell you red's better than blue
The press is fake news
I inherited a recession
I made our market expand, where do you see compression?
Business lessons from a senator
And before, I made out stocks come back tenfold
We're so nice in DC, oh please
You're so polite
You've been trying to talk over me all night
And here's something, Mr. Quid Pro Joe,
Don't talk to me about age, I mean, come on bro,
You think I'm scared of Covid?
You're seventy seven
That's basically on a gurney to Heaven!
Kamala Harris not good enough to president but still not too
 bad that much is evident
Biden, pretendin' he's all right (an') losing this segment
By the time this debate is over we'll all be residents
In an insane asylum, 'cause this is
An abomination and this is
Ridiculous

Wallace:
Excuse me?
I'd say take a walk, but it's like I'm not even here. This
 certainly was an eventful evening.

"Celebration" by J. Ramirez, 16, Philadelphia

So much pain has happened this year. I couldn't find something good until it was announced that Joe Biden had won the presidency. I was watching the celebrations and there were so many people who finally felt like they could breathe easy for the first time in four years.

"A Progressive's Food Diary Of Election Week" by Sarina Patel, 17, Tampa, Florida

nov. 1, breakfast

Coffee. Cubed potatoes. Congressional gridlock. Frying my hair straight before the road trip, I notice the flat iron snaps warmly to life, like a bottlecap. I think of Coca-Cola bottles showcased in museums, the red gowns and sugar behind hollow glass, the magic imprisoned. My college friend texts: I miss old soft drinks, and presidents. I text back: New campaign strategy—Make America Magical Again. It would sell.

nov. 2, dinner

At the restaurant in Atlanta, my friend shouts for beBEEdas and enCHEELadas. Her Spanish limps confidently, like wedding guests awful at dancing. We glue ourselves to salsa and chips and CNN and Instagram, constantly refreshed and exhausted. In the room, we binge-watch "Euphoria", attaching ourselves to the shiniest diversion from our collapsing democracy.

nov. 3, dessert

Biden miscalculated and lost Florida. Refusing to lock ourselves in, we grab dessert: Oreo cheesecake fudge.

nov. 4, breakfast

My friend and I share a grilled cheese in the park, watching the sky and polls turn blue. We discuss "victory," knowing things won't really change. They're all establishment Dems cut from the same flag: clones of cerulean. "You should run someday," my friend offers. The silence is so indulgent, I laugh.

nov. 5, breakfast

We spear popcorn chicken and mac and cheese, both dry and orange, with plastic forks. We glide through Publix, whispering nevadanevadanevada. The prayer ends on a vowel every time, so it feels unfinished. "I know fifth-graders who could count ballots faster than them fools," my friend complains, mouth full. She's right.

nov. 6, lunch

We discuss the Percy Jackson effect, or how Arizona turned blue. My friend gets four pumps of creamer in her coffee—no "Biden 2024" symbolism, she's just a caffeine addict. Driving home, I watch the hotel fade to a bump on the blue horizon: a distance I could never put between myself and politics.

nov. 7, lunch

Chipotle burrito bowls. A Republican relative tells me he voted blue. Cousins, friends, neighbors—staunch conservatives are coming out of the woodwork to vote blue. Still, I watch my friend mouth the truth through the rearview mirror: D-N-B (Dems Need Better). And then they call it.

nov. 7, late night snack

Gas station brownie ice cream brings limited catharsis, the ennui of choosing the lesser evil. We won. Yay. Driving into Florida, we spot a KFC. "Finger lickin' good!" barks the neon sign. Inside our gut the sugary feeling settles: disgusting, messy, artificially-flavored.

"Upholding Morals in a Hateful Time" by Eugene Sullivan, 17, Los Angeles

I donned my light brown steel toe boots in preparation for what I thought would be a violent performance by demonstrators who believed the integrity of the presidential election had been violated. My political beliefs do not align with those of the demonstrators, and I knew before I left my home for the protest that the mission would be an infiltration of sorts.

I felt a snowballing anxiousness as I got closer and closer to the demonstration. What I consume on social media has led me to believe that the "other side" consists of people who are irrational, violent, and hateful towards anyone that is not white or heterosexual.

The pathetic reality is that before attending this, my only conception of what an open Trump supporter could be was what I had been fed on social media. I was prepared to watch a pool of expressively hateful people grow angrier and angrier until they began destroying public property.

My expectations were completely incorrect.

What I did see was a pool of people happy in each other's company, dancing, singing, and fighting for what they loved. I realized that it is easy to feel good about hateful ideals when everyone around you is upholding the same hateful ideals.

Oct. 14

My father sealed the envelope and scrutinized it assiduously, making sure he completed all of the necessary steps. I waited impatiently, wanting him to get it done. But I could feel the sense of eagerness in the kitchen. I shivered. This was it.

He smiled, handed me the envelope, and led me out the door.

The air was sweet, refreshingly cold, holding its breath.

We turned the corner and there it stood. The mailbox stared at us with intensity, its sublime figure outlined by the streetlight beside it. I laughed in my head. It was like we were supposed to bow down to it.

We spoke just a few words. Something had silenced us. Something so much bigger than ourselves, something that stifled any talk about trivial matters.

I held his ballot tightly. It was just us outside, but I gripped it so that no one could take it away.

The ballot was thumping in my hand, the heartbeat of democracy. It echoed through both of us, beating a sacred drum.

It was dark out; the night had cloaked everything with its black robe, everything except for the sidewalk in front of us. The path to the mailbox was clear, illuminated by a different kind of light.

A flame that no one could put out. A flame that had burned for centuries, that had given warmth to the masses who marched for freedom.

I looked at the ballot. How much blood was spilled so that it could be there, in my hand?

We neared the mailbox. My father nodded towards it. "Slip it in."

I carefully pushed it into the box, watching it disappear forever. He looked at me, and we quietly headed home. I looked back. There was a bridge behind us. Edmund Pettus. There was a hill in front of us. Acropolis. I looked at my feet. We were walking on a bloody, scarred, chained, beaten, divided, wicked land.

They call it America.

And I have never been more proud

Then to have walked to the mailbox

Slip in his ballot

And say

That land is mine, too.

CONFRONTING A CHANGING CLIMATE

"i wake up to an orange sky."

"Noxious Air" by Matthew Coyle, 14, Eureka, California

I took this picture with my phone in my home in Humboldt County while wildfires raged nearby early in September. The air was toxic so you had to wear a mask when you went outside.

"colors" by Laura Ma, 16, Fremont, California

colors.

like a cascade of crow wings melting like iron, vertigo is splintering—concatenating with electrons and lightning. the sky trembles in flashes as a million bolts strike the clouds. i text my friends who have awakened from thunder, their pinging replies pulsating under my thumb—generations marveling at the first thunderstorm in 29 years. 5 a.m. silent sparrowsong: i fall asleep to august skies gilded in premature winter storms. i fall asleep to dreams of rain falling on dry, golden hills as lightning sets them ablaze. i wake up to an orange sky, forming wintery shadows in my room, i wake up to thirty-four zoom tiles of classmates, their blinds sickly tinted in pale pumpkin filters in september. how fitting it is that our u.s. history teacher lectures about the calvinist doom that ruined our puritan ancestors to form a compact of fear—not enlightened democracy—to survive in the massachusetts wilderness of 1620. unknown and haunted by the past and future. the same reactionary questions to bestow on citizens living under pumpkin skies 400 years later. minister jonathan edwards asks sinners in 1741 if they can already feel the afterlife burning. i am not a sinner nor a saint. yet there are flames from the sky. wisps of smoke weaving in and out of the spaces between the leaves in my garden. dust of a scorched earth blanketing the tiles of my spanish-style house and the windows of the family car. i pray for rain instead.

rain comes on november 8th, 2020.

My parents are considering euthanizing a family of raccoons.

The fires in California have made it so the raccoons have nowhere to turn for food other than our new lawn. For a month, we have covered the lawn with chili powder to repel their interest, but remain unsuccessful. My mom told me that the raccoon professionals would simply catch the raccoons then give them to the wildlife authorities. However, the fires have limited the available land to relocate them, ultimately leaving euthanization as the likely option.

My Grandpa is sick in the hospital. He doesn't have Covid-19, but his treatments have been thoroughly impacted by it. My Grandma hasn't been able to see him in weeks as he tries to get stronger. Thinking about him, and all the lives lost due to Covid-19, makes my heart wrench.

I started college two months ago. I live alone with my parents, as I did for most of high school since my siblings moved out. The excitement of starting college has worn off and I am left with the bleak reality that I spend every day alone, going to online school in a different time zone.

When they told me that the raccoons might be euthanized, I went to my room and thought. I don't love them, or even know them, yet the idea of them being killed made me feel the way I do when I acknowledge that I might never see my Grandpa again. It made me feel like I do every night when I remember that, after distracting myself all day, I am alone. Sometimes the tragedy of existing is as painful as that of not. I can't help that terrible thought arising when I remember the realities of the world we live in. A world where garbage eaters lose their homes because of fires and loneliness is the norm.

As people, we constantly feel the need to justify our actions. If we euthanize the raccoons, maybe things will be better where they end up. Maybe there will be platters of garbage and endless new lawns waiting to be destroyed. If we find a vaccine for the virus, maybe life will go back to normal. If I go to college, maybe I will be less lonely. Maybe we'll feel less guilty and miserable if we convince ourselves we're doing the right thing. Maybe not.

My parents are considering euthanizing a family of raccoons, and when euthanizing raccoons, you must not involve feelings, or else you too will fall into a deep existential spiral of wondering why grandpas get sick, people get lonely, and why life isn't always what you thought it would be.

Rest in peace.

"Beauty Outside My Window" by EllaRose Sherman, 14, Osprey, Florida

I did not want to spend all of quarantine in my room, so I started going to my backyard more. It was on one of these days outside, while I was reading, that I spotted a deer. Never in my entire life in Florida had I seen a deer. Florida has become so suburbanized that seeing any wildlife was rare, let alone something that majestic. It engraved itself in my mind, reminding me that there was still goodness in the world during these times.

Of course, I took some artistic liberties with this piece. Unfortunately, my window does not open to a sunlit forest, and my room is not this well-organized.

"Dear Generation Z" by Svanfridur Mura, 15, West Orange, New Jersey

Dear Generation Z, let us be the seeds
of the lodgepole pine.
Let us watch and wait as the kindling grows dry
and builds up beneath us.
Let us embrace the flames when they come,
when they burn down our parents.
Let us fall with the snapping branches of the old trees—
hear them splinter!
Let us crack open and burrow ourselves deep into
scorched earth.
Let us spread out our roots, watch as the worms turn
mother's body to dirt.
Let us sprout up from the ground and rejoice at the sun—
father's shadow is gone.
Let us grow fast and tall and sturdy and green now
that we have space.
Let us, when the old forest of this world implodes into wildfire,
melt off our wax skin
and eat their ashes
to grow anew.
Dear Generation Z, let us be the brave young people
who abandon the tribe.
Let us, when our elders dig their heels into the cracked earth
and choking dust,
turn our backs.
Let us leave them to their dogged worship of a withered past,
so they die.
Let us go out into the night with blistered feet and whining
stomachs and spirit
into swirling darkness.
Let us be unable to see home when the sun rises again,
just desert—
snake trails like shark fins.
Let us run through it, run and run and run and run, feet
sinking into sand.
Let us remember Eve, running with sweat carving canyons
down her ebony skin
abandoned, yet wise.

Let us forget all the rest of history! every heritage but that first
bite of knowledge.
Let us carry it out with us across the dunes until we reach the
river valley,
lone survivors.
crying naked to the stars
with jubilance.
Dear Generation Z, let me acknowledge
our tempestuous psyche.
I know that you are angry, that at night you simmer like the
roiling stars overhead—
I do too.
I know that you are tired, that exhaustion is a leech inside
your marrow sucking blood before
it's even made—
I am too.
I know that you are frightened, that your legs tremble like a
bewildered newborn fawn—
mine do too.
But we are the generation of crises.
We are the children of Covid-19.
We are the children of police brutality.
We are the children of raging inequity.
We are the children of political incompetence.
We are the children of the climate crisis.
We are 2020's children.
And we can cry, we can cover our eyes, we can gnash our
teeth with bitterness.
We can do all of those things, and still
abandon their foolishness and
use their burnt stumps as leverage
to rise from their ashes.

"Hypocrisy and Our Future" by Halle Tebbe, 16, Dublin, Ohio

While the pandemic has ravaged our country and the world, another issue that we as a nation and world have failed to work on is climate change. This year the Atlantic hurricane season was the most active on record, and record-breaking wildfires are currently burning the West Coast. This is an issue that will affect all of Generation Z. Why? Because we will be the ones responsible for the current inaction of our nation, of our world. We will be the ones to have to solve the disastrous consequences of climate change.

"Restoration" by Grace Song, 17, Great Neck, New York

after Camille T. Dungy

"Life is suffering. It is hard. The world is cursed. But still, you find reasons to keep on living."
—Princess Mononoke

After people died and everyone went home,

Kashmiri mountain goats in Wales captured a town

and paraded their victory. In Spain

Nubian ibexes descended from their mountain

and saw the ocean for the first time.

The Venice river exhaled sand and shells and shoals

of fish, and dolphins left saltwater, venturing

into canals. Cormorants dove with black-scaled wings,

scattered orange crabs. When hedgehogs

safely crossed London streets, Sika deer escaped

the Tokyo Zoo in search of adventure.

Baboons munched on India's streetgrass, and

pumas leapt over Brazil's brick walls. Hundreds

of Hawksbill sea turtles hatched on moon-silent shores.

There were African wild dogs, frolicking

on golf courses, and lions sleeping

in the middle of the road. Pronghorns

stampeding back to California; black bears

climbing Iowa trees again, their mouths

sweet with spring berries. Within months,

all the wild things returned. Rebirth, like wolves

released into Yellowstone. It's true

I want this scene today and forever:

clear rivers and unshakable mountains. Trees

straightening overhead and clouds

softening cliffs. Let me holdfast

to a flowering, fenceless land. Let me holdfast

to all the animals wandering, unafraid.

DISCOVERING

"I've welcomed the alone time."

"I'm Doing Yoga Now" by Linus Wood, 16, South Pasadena, California

Near the start of quarantine, I had to stop running because I had hurt my ankle, so my mom, who'd been doing yoga for years, got me into it.

Yoga has become one of the most fulfilling things in my life and I'll always remember 2020 as the year I started. It's all about mindfulness and strength and physicality (all things I'm obsessed with) and it's had such a positive effect on my mental and physical health. In this drawing I'm in a chair pose and stretching to my right, captured in a really dynamic angle. From that grounding you can go up through a checklist in your head, being mindful of everything that's happening in your body. ▶

"Never Truly Alone" by Evelyn Cox, 17, San Antonio, Texas

I've welcomed the alone time.

The number of things that I have learned or relearned about myself have made this a time of discovery. A time where I get to put my needs first. Where I can feel comfortable in my own skin for the entirety of a day, every day, a week, for months on end.

The state of being home and surrounded by the people and things I love most hasn't stopped the stress of school and college applications, or the feeling of helplessness when it comes to politics, or the full gravity of this deadly virus that flung us into this position. Being home has allowed me the time to recover and pick myself back up without the pressure of fitting in with my peers. It allowed me the space I needed to grow. ▶

January

August

Excerpts from "Self Expression" by Abram Loya, 18, Tacoma, Washington

The way I present myself via clothing has been my most prominent method of self expression, often a direct reflection of both my current mentality and my social well-being. Following images saved within my Snapchat memories, I recreated and captured about 100 of my own outfits throughout this year. Placing them in chronological order allows the viewer to see how quarantine affected the amount of effort I put into myself as my mental state fluctuated.

There is no notable change in my dress until about 30 images in. The start of quarantine in late March left me with a three-month adjustment period where the only times I left the house were for groceries. This did not change until I got a job in July. It's around here that you see me in a more presentable fashion more often.

By the end of the video, I had reached a new sense of self, which is visually apparent in my style.

See the video at https://www.youtube.com/watch?v=vNCIvl4-V7w

April

June

October

December

"Astrophotography From Home During Lockdown" by Griffin Haisman, 13, Providence, Rhode Island

In March of 2020, a sudden interest in the night sky was sparked in me. I ordered a tripod, then started using my Mom's DSLR camera and lens. I took pretty awful photos, but still, I was proud. I got better and better, staying up really late or waking up super early just to get more photos.

Eventually I got a star tracker, a device that counteracts the rotation of the earth to "follow" the stars through the sky. With that setup, from my light-polluted backyard of Providence, RI, I took some of my favorite photos to this day, including this picture of the moon.

I usually collect about 6 hours of exposure time on a target per night. I take all of those photos, stack them on top of each other to reduce noise, then use special software to get the image to how I like it. This whole process usually takes about 10 hours per photo.

One of the best aspects of astrophotography and astronomy is the community. Almost everyone into this hobby is willing to help each other out, and everyone is happy when anyone succeeds.

"External Reality vs. Internal Reality" by Steele Clevenger, 17, Portland, Oregon

A full-face mask to represent 2020, this piece symbolizes my external reality, shown on the left side of the image, juxtaposed with my internal reality, shown on the right side of the image.

My external reality depicts a city on fire, the fires which occurred during Black Lives Matter protests, as well as the wildfires which devastated the West Coast.

My internal reality depicts a quaint little house with a beautiful blue sky, a large sun, and rolling green hills—my inner calm, despite the chaos.

"Pink Hands" by Arianna Hellman, 16, New York City

How can anyone make a statement on beauty standards that has not been said a thousand times before? We all know that it should not matter what everyone else thinks. We all know that we should love ourselves. We also know that no matter how true these statements are, we don't listen to them. This is especially true for teenagers who spend every night scrolling through our social media feeds until we fall asleep.

When New York gave the orders to stay at home, I was in the midst of multiple eating disorders which had started the previous year. The idea of quarantine terrified me. I would have to try even harder to hide my worsening health from my family. I didn't want to get better.

As the days in quarantine blurred into weeks, all I was left with were my thoughts, I finally realized: "This is not what I want. I do not want this to become me." I began to confront my feelings, put effort into counseling, and find ways to express myself. The artwork that I created during the pandemic helped me to fully recover.

Each collage highlights a particular part of my body that made me feel insecure. I previously looked at myself as though in a clown mirror. My artwork, as well as my artistic process, transformed my self-doubt into beauty.

"Mind-Altering Light" by Lamiya Rangwala, 16, New Hyde Park, New York

We have to live in reality. But is it truly fixed? Or can looking at the world in a different way drastically change how we perceive reality?

When Covid-19 first hit, I was stressed and in despair. But soon, I started to view the coronavirus in a different light. I took a step back, shifted my perspective, and found that light. I realized nature was making a comeback. I was able to take a break from constant stress. My creativity was increasing. With so much time inside, I was finally able to do what I wanted, and it set me free. I wasn't held back by anyone else's opinions, and I found an escape into my own world.

"Little Great Moments" by Cathy Wang, 17, Claremont, California

I was scrolling through photos on my phone feeling nostalgic. These are four pictures I took before the pandemic, four "little great moments" I gravely miss. By using Photoshop, I drew myself in. This piece is about solitude, about embracing loneliness and learning to reflect.

But it also reflects the teenage experience of 2020. If there is one thing we know how to do, it is break boundaries: outdated ideological boundaries, cultural boundaries, and political boundaries. Here I try to break the boundaries between the real world and the digital world. The problems the world faces today require nonconventional solutions, and we are up for the task.

"Overcoming the Pandemic" by Chloe Kim, 14, Redmond, Washington

When we first went into lockdown, it felt like an extension of spring break. We laughed about the toilet paper shortage of 2020. We believed Covid-19 would disappear soon.

I remember the first couple of weeks thinking this was my chance to become stronger during quarantine and get a glow-up. I did YouTube workouts and workouts our coaches posted; I did much self-care and focused on myself. But as time went on, online school started, and the climbing season got canceled. I lost motivation and started falling into an unhealthy hole. My sleep schedule was nonexistent, and I rarely got off my bed, even for classes. I completely lost any desire to continue working out or do any self-care. I also stopped contacting my friends, which left me feeling so alone and weak. I felt like I was in this by myself, and no one could help me.

This signifies me finding my rhythm and becoming happier and finding a way to climb out of the hole and overcome my downward spiral.

"A Tight Grasp" by Sabine Croy, 17, Fort Wayne, Indiana

In a field of weeds at my house, I document my feelings of isolation.

I have never found comfort being around people. As a teenager in the midst of a worldwide pandemic, I have found eternal peace alone.

REFLECTING

"Please never forget how it felt."

"2020 Folded Us to Pieces" by Ayla Schultz, 17, Brooklyn

2020 folded me to pieces. Do you remember me gripping my bed sheets as the sirens went by? We could never have expected this: our world being beaten. Do you remember being trapped like that? The world was so quiet, so empty: the perpetual pounding of a city in shelter. Do you remember walking down the middle of Clinton, the way we charted the bike lanes of Brooklyn? The Empire State Building pulsed red, filling the sky with its spire. It caught the city's heartbeat and multiplied—do you remember the way it burned into our retinas, how we could not look away?

We wore down ourselves this year, sitting with our thoughts through March, April, May, June, July . . . . Can you feel how my heartbeat quickens, how I shrink away when the news is turned on. At night the neighbors blast CNN through their open windows. I would hear, "The total is now at 231,000. People are debating on when— if ever— this will be over." They said our city will never fully recover, that its stretch marks and scars will remain. Our city, made of glass and steel—the I-beam ridden capital of the world. I did not believe them; our city is capable of eternally shifting, the kinetic sand readjusting beneath our feet.

I am on 200, 200 days closed and the last thing I held there was a physics textbook. They say we will never fully recover, that our generation will hold the scars this time has forged. I hope that is not true, that we will not forget but forgive—and file the dead into our soul. Let this piece of us live on, let it join my curved spine and growing pains.

Please never forget how it felt to sit in my room and stare up at my skylight watching the clouds drift as we circle into the sun. My room filling up with light, the outside leaking in as I sit and wait.

I hope you remember how dry our hands were, how they cracked and trailed from all the soap. How it burned into our nose and caught our lungs. I planted a garden, if you recall, kneading life in tomatoes and squash as our foundations shook. I watched as they grew and blossomed, tying them to stakes as they arched towards the sky.

They asked me to think of the big questions, to talk of our future as everything fell on our head. They asked me about college, about essays and essays and The Test that never happened. They asked me to boil ourselves down into 650 words. We knew that was truly impossible, that no matter how small we make ourselves there will always be more words to occupy.

I hope that we are constantly evolving, that we are not the same person we are now—that we have left her in our small room in Brooklyn staring at the sky.

"Comic 2020" by Mikaela Edwards, 16, Sacramento, California

The events of 2020 could seriously qualify for its own comic. I got inspired by a comic I saw online—"Hip Hop Family Tree"—and gathered as many crazy and important events together as I could and put them into an almost humorous context.

The character in the middle represents the Top 100 music hits this year. Starting from the left, the other characters represent the US election, the pandemic, the Mars missions, a soldier who represents that World War III scare we had in the beginning of the year, a grieving Kobe Bryant fan, and a character representing the global wildfires, with the Australian flag tattooed on her leg because it was not just California and Oregon who suffered from the fires this year.

"Where Did the Year Go?" by Sofia Narvaez, 17, Longmont, Colorado

It's funny how we had all the time in the world at the start of the pandemic and yet it feels as though the entire year slipped right through our fingers and disappeared.

"If you could go back in time and erase Covid-19, would you?" by Maya Ferreira, 16, West Hartford, Connecticut

Yesterday I was doing what every teenager does when they're bored: I was scrolling through TikTok. I came across a video that really stuck out to me. The video simply asked, "If you could go back in time to March and erase Covid-19 but it would eliminate all the memories you've made the past 8 months, would you?"

My first instinct was to say yes. No more Covid, how much better can you get than that? But when my eyes hit the 53.7k comments, my mind suddenly went blank. People were arguing back and forth, who was right, who was wrong, why you shouldn't think something, why you should, and on and on and on and on. I finally scrolled past the video because I couldn't read it anymore.

The video is gone now. But—that's what happens, right? Teenagers now live in a world where if they don't want to listen to something, read something, or look at something, they can simply just scroll past it.

But what happens if we don't forget? I can't forget that video. I can't forget how one group of people told others that they were selfish for saying they wouldn't go back in time, saying that makes them responsible for 200k+ deaths, and another group of people saying those who would choose to go back are just scared of the future.

The truth is we've all lost something, given something up that we loved, got held back from opportunities. But what happened to being all in it together? What happened to being kind to one another? What happened to respecting each other's opinions?

Some may say that I'm selfish, but I wouldn't go back in time to erase Covid. Everything makes us who we are and teaches us what we know. What I now know is in an uncertain world, the only certainty is that opinions don't change opinions.

Opinions in an Uncertain World

I'm gonna delete it. No thinking. No preview. Delete. 10-17 — 6902
View replies (108)

Everything happens for a reason. COVID changed my life and it was a bit of a wake up call for me. 10-18 — 7562
View replies (33)

I love how much I've changed over quarantine but I would go back 100%, people lost their lives... a glow up doesn't compare to a life 10-18 — 2216
Liked by creator

also, thousands of people have died. THOUSANDS. if we went back, they could all come back. delete is the right choice 10-18 — 66
View replies (11)

200k deaths in only the u.s. Who's to say i cant make those memories again? Delete. 10-18 — 2870
View replies (33)

I would probably be selfish :(Covid helped me escape a toxic engagement, take the time to build my art business, clean up my life, and meet my bf 10-18 — 2040

U guys r like "well I wouldn't because I grew so much 😭" people DIED 10-18 — 1134
View replies (53)

I know some may think it's selfish but everything happens for a reason and even though covid brought death it also brought strength and change 10-17 — 17.1K
View replies (55)

181

ANSWER CHOICES

Pillow	Maine	Coon
Banana	America	Trend
Love	Bread	Picnics
Mask	Watermelon	Chai
Arepas	Positivity	TikTok
Yourself	Pumpkin	Masseur
Dreams	Stickers	Type A

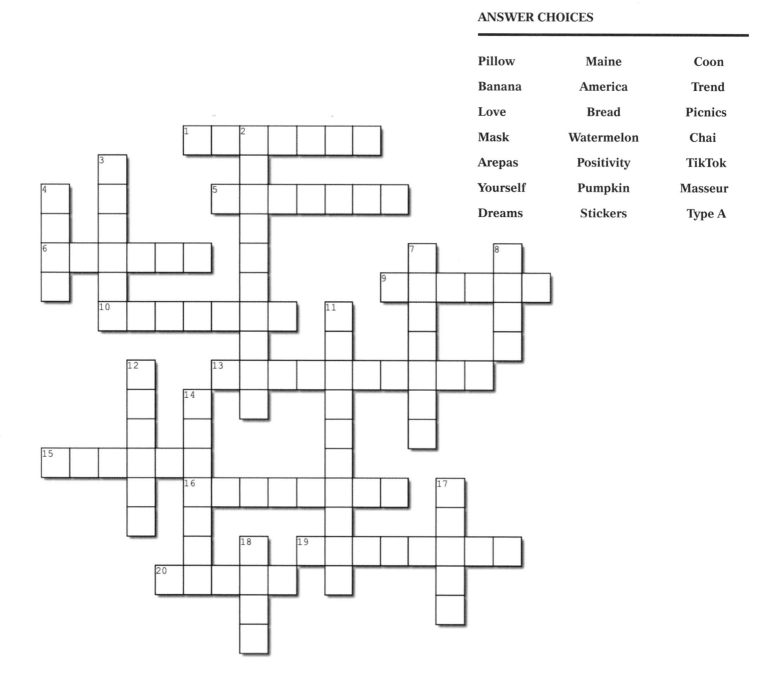

"To 2020, Humanity's Pause Button" by Valentina Avellaneda, 17, Houston

2020 tastes like orange juice after you've brushed your teeth: tangy, yet retaining a little bit of sweetness. Here's what I've learned, little delights I've experienced, and recipes that remind me of this year.

ACROSS

1. Opening a perfectly ripe _____. A softening moon that can still hold its shape.

3. Uncertainty is uncomfortable, but if a _____ person like me was able to navigate these past months through TikTok, calligraphy, and babysitting, you can too.

4. I hate gossiping, but love tea. And _____ is my favorite.

6. Having a personal cat _____.

8. _____ spiced lattes, which I've concluded my taste buds don't like.

12. Synonym for optimism. 2020 has tested humanity, but focusing on little delights has made it bearable.

15. I've spent so much time on _____ , and have learned that it's perfectly okay to not be productive all the time. It's not lazy to rest!

17. Recovering from an eating disorder has taught me the importance of self care: the only person you need to please and protect is _____.

18. Living my rainy day _____ : not having to leave the house, staying in pajamas.

DOWN

1. Garden focaccia _____ ! My baking magnum opus. My kitchen smelled of rosemary, dill, and red peppers; an edible floral garden.

2. Mom's _____ on Sunday mornings: a round patty made with white maize and a side of *huevos pericos* with *chocolate caliente*.

5. My cat isn't actually fat, he just had 5+ years worth of fur I hadn't brushed off. He also happens to be 90% _____ (according to a cat scanner).

7. _____ needs a little TLC, emphasis on loving care. Life isn't just about money and power, there are human feelings behind every immigrant our leaders criminalize.

8. _____. With anyone, any time. Red gingham blankets never fail to make me smile.

9. _____ is deceiving: a naive fruit picker like me can't tell the difference between an underripe, ripe, and overripe thirst quencher.

10. Little kids _____ me. Babysitting my siblings this summer released my inner child— I transformed into the *cookie monster, pizza man,* and *a guy named Joe*. I had no clue my dulcet voice could conjure such manly accents.

11. Peeling _____. The satisfaction in having no residue.

13. People who put on a _____ correctly.

14. The best feeling in the world: a cold _____ next to you when you're sleeping and your body heats up.

16. Banana bread: simple, versatile, comforting. When quarantine boredom hit, this _____ kept my oven busy.

ANSWERS

ACROSS
1. Banana
3. Type A
4. Chai
6. Masseur
8. Pumpkin
12. Positivity
15. Tiktok
17. Yourself
18. Dreams

DOWN
1. Bread
2. Arepas
5. Maine Coon
7. America
8. Picnics
9. Watermelon
10. Love
11. Stickers
13. Mask
14. Pillow
16. Trend

INDEX OF ARTISTS AND WORKS

ABOUT THE EDITOR

Katherine Schulten was editor-in-chief of The New York Times Learning Network from 2006 to 201e9 and is still a contributing editor there. She grew up in Texas and began her career in education right after college, with students in Brooklyn, New York. From there, she briefly taught in Japan, then spent 10 years as an English teacher at Brooklyn's Edward R. Murrow High School, where she was also advisor to the school newspaper.

After winning a Prudential Fellowship to the Columbia School of Journalism, Katherine worked for nine years in schools all over the city as a literacy consultant for the New York City Writing Project. In that role she focused on Career and Technical Education, helping teachers infuse writing into subjects across the curriculum, from science and math to plumbing and cosmetology.

Katherine lives in Brooklyn with her husband and is the mother of twins now in their twenties.